Soap & Cosmetic
Labeling

How to Follow
THE RULES AND REGS
Explained in Plain English

Marie Gale

Cinnabar Press

Broadbent, Oregon

Soap and Cosmetic Labeling

2nd edition

How to Follow the Rules and Regs Explained in Plain English

by Marie Gale

Published by:

Cinnabar Press
PO Box 39
Broadbent, OR 97414

Notice of Rights

Notice of Liability

Updates / Errata

To report any errors in this book, please send a note to errata@mariegale.com. Also check www.mariegale.com/labeling for updates to this book, links to state and federal code and other sites of interest.

ISBN 978-0-9795945-1-9

Table of Contents

Chapter 2

Is it a Cosmetic, a Soap or Something Else?....13

What Goes On the Label?

Chapter 3

Understanding the Package & Label 23

Chapter 5
Business Name & Address 39

Chapter 6
Quantity ofContents...........................41

Chapter 7

The Ingredient Declaration 63

Chapter 10

Ingredient Declaration: Special Circumstances 93

Chapter 11

Required Warning Statements 99

Preface

As handcrafters and small business owners making soaps, cosmetics, candles and similar products in the US, we're pretty lucky. Even though we might sometimes complain about the time and effort it takes to understand and comply with the rules, most products in the US are still "self-regulated".

Unlike those living in many other countries, we don't have to get approval beforehand; the FDA and other agencies still operate on the basis that we'll do our best to comply with the rules. After all, the rules and regs are written with the intent to protect and inform the consumer.

As long as handcrafters and small businesses continue to make a sincere effort to understand and follow the required federal and state guidelines, there is less likelihood that more stringent regulations and enforcement will be considered necessary by "the powers that be".

To that end, I hope this book helps you to understand and comply with the regulations for your product(s), thereby allowing all of us to enjoy an industry self-regulated for as long as possible.

I also hope that it provides enough information that soap and cosmetic handcrafters can save their precious time by not having to wade through all the regulations personally and not having to enter into long discussion with other handcrafters trying to figure out what they mean.

Acknowledgements

First, my daughter, Elizabeth Gale. Not only is she a marvelous and talented person (no prejudice here!), she also spent many hours compiling all the information about the state regulations and putting it into brief but understandable form. And she did all that while working full-time, going to college and taking care of my very precious grandson.

Second, Jeré for his support, excellent advice and kindness while I was in the throes of deadlines and typesetting. I can't imagine how I would have gotten through without his help.

Last, Desi, who gave me some excellent editing comments and was kind enough to give up hours to go through my drafts with a fine tooth comb and Joan and Susan, who helped immensely with their editing skills on the first and second editions respectively.

Marie Gale

Introduction

There are many agencies and government bodies at both the state and federal levels that enforce hundreds of rules and regulations about how products should be packaged and labeled in order to protect and inform the American consumer. What I found through all my research is that getting the labeling right isn't very *complicated* ... but it is very *detailed.*

Who this book is for

This book is written for people who are making soap, cosmetics, candles and ancillary products as homecrafters or in a small business. It's intended as a help in cutting through the many, many, many pages of print and electronic material that outline what is needed to comply with the rules and regs about packaging and labeling.

What this book covers

The contents of this book are intended to provide an easily understandable guide to labeling requirements for the handcrafting of soaps, cosmetics, candles and similar products. It covers most things that are likely to come up in making typical labeling decisions about what must go on your label, the format of the information, where it should be placed and the size of the text.

While all consumer products have some general labeling requirement, cosmetics have some very detailed regulations. You'll need to determine what kind of product you have and which labeling requirements fit - all of which you should be able to do as you go through this book.

In addition to the actual labeling guidelines for cosmetics and some home products, there are some sections on color additives, ingredients and other information that will be of use in finalizing the content of your labels and packaging.

The book does not include information on labeling drugs or medical devices, foods or items that fall under the purview of the EPA.

2nd Edition

This 2nd Edition, published in early 2008, contains additional clarification and diagrams based on the questions received from readers. There is also a new chapter (Chapter 9) specifically addressing ingredient declarations for soap.

More Info

This book has a website! *www.mariegale.com/labeling*

Updates and errata for the book will be posted there along with links to the various government and other sites listed or mentioned in the book.

You'll need the ISBN number from the back of the book or copyright page in order to access the page(s) specifically for owners of the book.

Section 1

Products

and the

Authority Over Them

Chapter 1
Who Makes The Rules?

Labeling and packaging rules generally come in the form of federal or state regulations (or laws). In most cases they were originally created to protect consumers and/or the environment in some fashion or another.

There are several different sets of rules and laws, each of which is administered or enforced by a different local, state or federal agency. The determination of which laws apply and which agency or bureau is responsible is generally determined by the type of the product and the geographic area it is produced in and/or shipped through.

Federal Authority

The Federal Government has many different agencies that oversee products being sold to consumers. However, the good news is that only a few of them have authority over soaps, cosmetics and other products often made along with them. The bad news is that sometimes it's hard to determine which rules apply.

Federal Trade Commission (FTC)

The Federal Trade Commission (FTC) is the agency that is supposed to protect the American consumer from unfair or deceitful business practices. They have many areas of responsibility, but the one that applies most directly to those making and labeling soaps and home products are the regulations that require disclosure to the consumer of the actual contents of the package, what it is and who makes it.

The FTC specifically deals with "consumer commodities" that are not cosmetics or drugs. A consumer commodity is defined as:

Any article, product, or commodity of any kind or class which is customarily produced or distributed for sale through retail sales of various kinds for consumption or use by individuals for the purpose of personal care or in the performance of services ordinarily rendered within the household, and which is typically consumed or expended in the course of such use.

In other words, a consumer commodity is something that is purchased retail, used by an individual in the course of their daily life and generally used up at some point.

Examples of consumer products include: potpourri, candles, hair brushes, clothing, toilet paper, furniture polish, garden tools, air fresheners, fabric softener and greeting cards. Under most conditions, soap is a consumer commodity. (See Chapter 2 for more details.)

Fair Packaging and Labeling Act (FPLA)

The FPLA is a set of laws that apply to labeling and packaging. It was written to ensure that packages and their labels provide consumers with accurate information about what the product is, how much product is actually in the package (quantity of contents), who made or distributed the product and to make it easier for the consumer to do value comparisons.

With a few exceptions, the FPLA applies to ALL consumer products (except foods, drugs and cosmetics) and requires:

a) a statement identifying the commodity, (i.e. detergent, sponges, etc.);

b) the name and place of business of the manufacturer, packer, or distributor; and

c) the net quantity of contents in terms of weight, measure, or numerical count (measurement must be in both metric and inch/pound units).

Enforcement

The Federal Trade Commission has authority over the enforcement of the FPLA, at least on a broad basis. Their website includes places for people to make complaints and get information about various products.

Companies that produce products that have been determined to be unsafe or incorrectly (fraudulently) labeled can be required to issue product recalls.

Food and Drug Administration (FDA)

The Food and Drug Administration has the responsibility to oversee all foods, drugs and cosmetics. Their responsibility and action for each of these three areas is different.

All drugs and medical devices must be approved by the FDA. The FDA is also responsible for watching drugs and medical devices that are imported to ensure they meet all US regulations.

For foods, the FDA particularly oversees and approves food additives (especially colors) and is responsible for the safety of the foods on the market. Anything that can be ingested comes under the responsibility of the FDA, including vitamin supplements.

Cosmetic regulation under the FDA mainly covers color additives, what can (and can't) be used in a cosmetic, and labeling requirements to keep the consumer informed.

Federal Food, Drug & Cosmetic Act

The FDA's primary authority comes from the Federal Food, Drug and Cosmetic (FD&C) Act of 1938, as amended. (Think protecting the public from snake oil salesmen!) This act details all the laws that concern foods, drugs, medical devices and cosmetics.

When the Fair Packaging and Labeling Act was written, the responsibility for its implementation for foods, drugs, medical devices and cosmetics was delegated to the FDA and enacted through the Federal Food Drug and Cosmetic Act (FD&C Act). Generally, all of the requirements of the FPLA as applied to packaging and what must be included on a package are included as part of the Food, Drug and Cosmetic Act.

The purpose of the FD&C Act is:

> *To protect consumers from unsafe or deceptively labeled or packaged products by prohibiting the movement in interstate commerce of adulterated or misbranded food, drugs, devices and cosmetics.*

The FD&C Act covers all aspects of foods, drugs and cosmetics. For cosmetics specifically it covers labeling, ingredient lists, color additives, warning labels, and the truthful and safe presentation of the cosmetics to the public.

However, the authority of the FDA is technically only authorized to **prevent movement in interstate commerce** of products that are **adulterated** or **misbranded.**

The key terms of "adulterated" and "misbranded" need to be well understood as they form the basis of all FDA authority and regulation. It is only by being adulterated or misbranded AND travelling through interstate commerce that a product can be in violation of the law with regard to the FDA.

Adulterated

A cosmetic is considered adulterated if:

a) it contains a substance which may make the product harmful to consumers under customary conditions of use;

b) it contains a filthy, putrid, or decomposed substance;

c) it is manufactured or held under insanitary[1] conditions whereby it may have become contaminated with filth, or may have become harmful to consumers; or

d) it is not a hair dye and it contains a non-permitted color additive.

---

[1] insanitary: So unclean as to be a likely cause of disease.

Misbranded

A cosmetic is misbranded if:

a) its labeling is false or misleading;

b) it doesn't bear the required labeling information; or

c) the container is made or filled in a deceptive manner.

It is important to note that labeling may be considered misleading if what is said on the label is deceptive OR if an important fact is left off the label.

It is also considered to be misbranded if the product name uses or suggests the name of one ingredient but not the others, even though the full ingredient list is on the package. (See Chapter 4 for details.)

"Labeling" includes all labels and other written, printed or graphic material on or accompanying a product, including statements made on a website promoting or selling the product.

Color Additives

The FDA has exclusive authority over color additives that may be used in food, drugs or cosmetics. They regulate not only what color additives may be used, but what they may be used for and sometimes how much can be used in a particular product.

Full information on color additives can be found in Chapter 13 and Appendix A.

Enforcement

The FDA has authority to enforce all aspects of the FD&C Act. Their powers include the right to inspect premises and products, confiscate products, issue public warnings, issue recall notices, restrain a company from doing business, and/or filing criminal charges for non-compliance.

National Institute of Standards and Technology

The National Institute of Standards and Technology is an agency of the US Department of Commerce. They provide a variety of products and services to U.S. industry and the public in collaboration with NIST laboratories, federal agencies, national measurement institutes, state and local governments, and the private sector.

Within the NIST is the Division of Weights and Measures which, through the National Conference of Weights and Measures (NCWM), publishes a handbook each year containing their recommended Uniform Laws and Regulations with regard to weights and measures.

Uniform Laws and Regulations

The purpose of these Uniform Laws and Regulations is:

> *To achieve, to the maximum extent possible, standardization in weights and measures laws and regulations among the various States and local jurisdictions in order to facilitate trade between the States, permit fair competition among businesses, and provide uniform and sufficient protection to all consumers*

The Uniform Laws and Regulations include, among other things, a Uniform Weights and Measures Law and a set of Uniform Packaging and Labeling Regulations. They are written in such a way that any state can adopt all or part for inclusion in its state law. The idea is for all states to adopt similar regulations so that it is less confusing for businesses and consumers.

Uniform Weights and Measures Laws (UWML)

The Uniform Weights and Measures Law (UWML) deals with setting up a system to verify the accuracy of and to certify scales used to weigh consumer products. It also includes provisions to check consumer packages to ensure the weights stated on them are accurate.

The law recommends the establishment of a State Weights and Measures Division with the authority to enforce the rules. Suggested activities of the proposed State Weights and Measures Division include checking and verifying or certifying scales and measuring devices (and charging a fee of some kind for doing so) and granting "Special Police Powers" which entitle them to enter any commercial premises, issue stop-use orders, seize product and stop any commercial vehicle to inspect the contents and review documentation.

California, for example, has adopted part of these rules and has laws now that require that all scales used to weigh commercial products be certified by an inspector (for a fee, of course). The inspections are managed out of county offices.

Uniform Packaging and Labeling Regulations (UPLR)

The Uniform Packaging and Labeling Regulations (UPLR) provide specific guidelines for labeling products to be sold to the consumer. The UPLR details implementation of all the requirements of the FPLA and is designed to be enforced at a state level.

Environmental Protection Agency (EPA)

The EPA has jurisdiction over any products that claim to kill or repel insects or rodents. All pesticides, herbicides, and rodenticides fall under their jurisdiction. Their regulation and approval process is intended to control heavy-duty, potentially toxic substances, but any claim to repel insects falls under the EPA.

A product that would normally be considered a cosmetic and under the jurisdiction of the FDA, such as a body lotion, falls under EPA jurisdiction as soon as a claim to repel insects is made.

In most cases the product and label must be approved by the EPA before the product is placed on the market. There is a small window of exclusion for biological-based insecticides (i.e. Citronella and some other essential oils). In order to qualify within that window, both the active and inert (inactive) ingredients must fall within a restricted list and the labeling must comply with all EPA rules.

This book does not address the labeling requirements for products which claim to repel insects.

US Department of Agriculture (USDA)

The USDA is responsible for overseeing products for agricultural crops and animals (but not items for pet care). For some strange reason, horse shampoos and grooming items fall within pet care.

The USDA is also responsible for regulating the use of the term "organic" and overseeing organic certification, even for cosmetic items.

State Authority

While the FDA and FTC have federal authority, and therefore authority over products that travel through inter-state commerce, each state has authority within its own state. If the product is made and sold in a state or just passes through it, any State regulations apply in addition to the federal regulations.

All states, with the exception of Rhode Island, have some kind of Weights and Measures Law, most of which are based on the federal recommended standards from the NCWM.

All states, with the exception of North Dakota, have adopted some version of the Uniform Packaging and Labeling requirements.

In addition, some states have laws directly and specifically applicable to the packaging and labeling of soaps, cosmetics and other similar handcrafted items. Florida, for example, requires inspection and certification of facilities making cosmetics, although most states do not.

See Appendix E for a summary of the information about each state, including contact information, notes about existing state laws and links to pertinent documents.

County & City Authority

County regulations, if they exist, usually cover licensing and/or inspection. In some cases the states delegate enforcement of the Uniform Weights and Measures Law to county officials.

While not every county has regulations in addition to the state rules, it's still a good idea to see if there are any applicable county laws or other governing agencies for your location.

Some cities and towns also have licensure regulations that might affect production facilities, although it's unlikely that they would have product labeling rules or laws.

Summary

The fundamental idea behind of all these laws and the regulations that enforce them is to ensure that manufacturers provide adequate and correct information to consumers and don't sell contaminated or dangerous products.

Of course, the devil is in the details and those devilish details are what this book is all about.

Chapter 2

Is it a Cosmetic, a Soap or Something Else?

The type of product and its intended use determine the labeling requirements, the applicable regulations and the ruling authority. However, figuring out exactly what the product IS can be a challenge in itself. The key is in the intended use.

Intended Use

The intended use is determined by what is said on all the labels and other written, printed or graphic matter on or accompanying the product. This includes labels, inserts, risers, display packs, leaflets, promotional literature or any other written or printed information distributed with a product, including statements made on a website to describe or promote the product.

The courts, in deciding what kind of product it is and what regulations apply, have relied more on what the consumer thinks the label statements mean and less on what the labeler or regulatory agency thinks they mean.

So even if you try to slide by with very carefully worded materials and labels, it may not matter. If the consumer comes away thinking that your product will cure their arthritus or clear up acne or make their eczema go away—even if you didn't actually say so—then the product could be considered a drug.

Cosmetics

A cosmetic is a product intended to exert a physical, and not a physiological[1], effect on the human body. The FDA definition of a cosmetic is:

> *A product, except soap, intended to be applied to the human body for cleansing, beautifying, promoting attractiveness or altering the appearance.*

So if a product cleanses the body, it's a cosmetic (except if it's just soap, which is covered below). If a product "makes skin appear smoother" (and therefore more beautiful), it's a cosmetic. If it makes you prettier, it's a cosmetic. If it makes your hair shiny and clean, it's a cosmetic. If it makes your skin "glow", it's a cosmetic, but if it claims to heal pimples, then it's a drug.

Examples of cosmetic products:

Bubble bath, bath salts, shampoo, make-up of all kinds, hair dye, mascara, nail polish, body powder, body oil, hand lotion, face cream, foot lotion, body spritzer, perfume, face toner, cuticle cream, salt scrub, sugar scrub, exfoliants, clay masks, shaving cream, after-shave and feminine deodorant products.

Cosmetic Ingredients

The raw materials used as ingredients of cosmetic products are also considered to be cosmetics.

That means that the packaging and labeling of a container of shea butter, if it is to be used as an ingredient in a cosmetic, must follow the same labeling requirements for a cosmetic.

If you purchase a cosmetic ingredient from a supplier, the supplier must provide all the appropriate information for that ingredient just like any other cosmetic. Generally that includes the name of the ingredient or a list of ingredients of the product if it is already blended (and which includes sufficient information to add it to your cosmetic label). The ingredient name(s) must be in the correct

---

[1] **physiological**: Having to do with all the functions of a living organism or any of its parts.

format (see Chapter 7). The supplier should also be able to supply a Material Safety Data Sheet (MSDS) for the product.

Drugs

A drug is defined as:

> *A product that is intended for use in the cure, mitigation, treatment, or prevention of disease and articles intended to affect the structure or any function of the body.*

Drugs range from the obvious (antibiotics, hypertension medication or novocaine) to the not so obvious (toothpaste with fluoride, dandruff shampoo, anti-perspirant deodorant and sunblock).

In the grey area are products that somewhat innocently act like drugs. Surgical anesthesia or a prescription painkiller are easily recognizable as drugs. It's less apparent, but still true, that a product containing an essential oil that "relieves pain" or "reduces stress" could be construed to be a drug depending on how it is presented to the consumer.

Food

Any product that specifically claims to be "edible" is classed as a food and must be labeled as such. A body powder made of food grade tapioca starch and honey powder may contain all edible ingredients, but if the claim is made that it is edible, then it changes from being a cosmetic to a food and all the labeling rules change with that distinction.

Stating that a cosmetic is "non-toxic" and therefore could be ingested without harm is not the same as claiming that the product is edible—unless the consumer feels that the intended use is to ingest the product, in which case it becomes a food based on the intended use perceived by the consumer.

Both a Drug AND a Cosmetic

A product can be both a drug and a cosmetic. If it is intended to cleanse, beautify or promote attractiveness AND treat or prevent disease or otherwise affect the structure or any function of the human body, then it is both a cosmetic and a drug.

Toothpaste is a good example of a product that is frequently both a cosmetic and a drug. It is intended to clean the teeth and make them more attractive (cosmetic), but it often contains fluoride to prevent cavities (drug).

Any product that qualifies as a drug (whether or not it also qualifies as a cosmetic) must be treated and labeled as a drug.

Soap

Something that is called and recognized as "soap" can be either a cosmetic or a consumer commodity, depending on what it is made of and how it is marketed.

Soap as a Consumer Commodity

The FDA definition of soap is:

> *A product in which the non-volatile portion consists principally of an alkali salt of fatty acids.*

In other words, it's the result of mixing an alkali (usually sodium hydroxide or potassium hydroxide) with fatty acids (animal or vegetable fats or oils or derivitives thereof).

It is important to note that the definition says it is "principally" an alkali salt of fatty acids. Adding extra ingredients to a soap that which do not significantly change it does not violate the definition of soap. You can add color, scent, foam enhancers, stabilizers, fillers or other ingredients to a soap and it would still fall within the definition of soap.

The Food, Drug and Cosmetic Act specifically exempts soap. To be exempt from FDA regulation, the product must be a soap based on the FDA definition, must be labeled "soap" and make no other claims than that it "cleanses" or "cleans". Soap which is exempt from FDA regulations is considered a consumer commodity and must follow the FTC Fair Labeling and Packaging Act requirements.

Soap as a Cosmetic

If the soap labeling makes any cosmetic claims (such as "moisturizing", "deodorizing", "skin softening", etc.) then it is considered a cosmetic and must comply with all cosmetic labeling requirements.

Cosmetic claims can be on the front panel of the label (i.e. "Moisturizing Body Soap"), on an informational panel of the label (i.e. "this soap moisturizes as it cleans"), in the ingredient statement (i.e. "glycerine (moisturizer)"), or in any promotional materials, advertising or web copy about the soap. It doesn't matter where they are made—if the consumer (or the FDA) comes away with the idea that the product will have cosmetic benefits, then it is a cosmetic.

A synthetic detergent-based product may be labeled as "soap" but since it does not meet the technical definition of "soap" as stated in the regulations, it is considered a cosmetic and must be labeled according to cosmetic labeling standards. Check the labels for typical "soap" bars in the grocery store or pharmacy, and you'll see that many include the ingredients, even though they area called "soap". That's because most of them are actually synthetic detergent bars, not true soap by the FDA definition.

For those who make and sell soap products using a melt and pour soap base, it is important to find out the actual ingredients of the base being used. If it is "a product in which the non-volatile portion consists principally of an alkali salt of fatty acids," then it is a soap. If it made of a synthetic detergent base, it is not actually soap, it's a cosmetic. If in doubt, check with the manufacturer or distributor and get a definitive answer in writing for your records.

Consumer Commodities

As mentioned earlier, the definition of a "consumer commodity" is:

Any article, product, or commodity of any kind or class which is customarily produced or distributed for sale through retail sales of various kinds for consumption or use by individuals for the purpose of personal care or in the performance of services ordinarily rendered within the household, and which is typically consumed or expended in the course of such use.

In other words, a consumer commodity is something that is purchased retail, used by an individual in the course of their daily life and is generally used up at some point.

For the most part, consumer commodities are not applied to the body in a way that they might be absorbed (as in cream, lotion, deodorant, drugs, vitamins or food).

Examples of consumer commodities:

Candles, wax melts, room fresheners, linen sprays, smelly-jelly, drawer sachets, potpourri and closet deodorizers are all non-cosmetic consumer commodities. So are household cleaning products including dish soap, laundry detergent, furniture polish and car care products.

Not Consumer Commodities

Non-consumable items are not classed as consumer commodities for the purposes of the FPLA. By definition, a consumer commodity gets used up. Other items that do not get used up are generally not considered consumer commodities for the purposes of the FPLA, even though they are sold to a consumer. Many non-consumables are regulated by other agencies and regulations. These are not covered in this book.

Examples of non-consumables:

Jewelry, soap dishes, candle holders, textile materials, greeting cards, paper, pictures, photo albums, souvenirs, toys, woodenware.

18

Pet Care Products

Animal care and grooming products (which might be considered be "animal cosmetics") aren't covered by the FDA. They are also excluded from being classed as a "consumer commodity", so are not covered by the FPLA.

Generally, however, they are covered by some sort of state regulations concerning packaging and labeling.

Insect Repellent

As noted in Chapter 1, any product that claims to repel or kill insects falls under the purview of the EPA (and must be labeled in accordance to EPA insecticide labeling regulations and requirements).

Most products that claim to repel or kill insects must be approved by the EPA before being marketed, although biological products made using only ingredients from preapproved lists may be sold without pre-approval.

So, What Is It?

You can tell if it's soap by how it's made. If it's made with lye, water and oils, then it's soap. If you call your product "soap" and just say that it cleans then it is a consumer commodity, not a cosmetic.

If your soap base is made with synthetic detergents, it is a cosmetic (even if you only call it "soap").

If you list any cosmetic qualities for your soap, other than that it cleanses, it is a cosmetic.

If the product is intended to clean, beautify, promote attractiveness or alter appearance, then it's a cosmetic.

If the product is not applied to the body, but is used to enhance the environment (candles or room fresheners, for example) then it is not a cosmetic, it is a consumer commodity.

If the product is intended to cure, treat, mitigate or prevent disease or to affect the function or structure of the body, then it's a drug, regardless of how it is applied.

If the product is marketed as "edible" and/or is intended to be eaten, then it is a food. That includes body cosmetics that are "edible".

In most cases, the intent of the product and how it is presented to the consumer is the determining factor.

For example, an additive to a vaporizer could be:

> » a **drug** if it is promoted to "clear the sinuses" or "make breathing easier",

> » a **consumer commodity** if it claims to "make the house smell nice."

> » a **cosmetic** if it "makes pores appear smaller"

A hand lotion scented with a blend of essential oils is a cosmetic even if that esssential oil blend happens to repel insects. However, if a claim is made that it repels insects, then it is an insecticide (and must be labeled in accordance with the EPA regulations).

It is all in what the product does, how the product is promoted to the consumer and what the consumer thinks is the intended use of the product.

Section 2

What Goes On the Label?

Chapter 3

Understanding the Package & Label

Before trying to address the specifics of what goes on a label, it is important to understand the package and the label in general.

Professional Cosmetic Products

Cosmetic labeling requirements only apply to cosmetics which are sold directly to consumers. Professional cosmetic products, such as items used exclusively by beauticians or cosmeticians in beauty salons and not sold to consumers, are not required to follow the cosmetic labeling requirements. However, if professional products are also sold at retail, then they are consumer commodities.

Those little shampoos, conditioners and lotions placed in hotel rooms for the guests are not consumer cosmetics.

Free samples are not consumer cosmetics.

A product that is given as a "free gift" with purchase is a consumer cosmetic because the "gift" is only available when another product is purchased.

A product that is labeled as a "free sample" or "for professional use only" but is also sold as a retail product, is still a consumer cosmetic, even when you give it away for free.

In other words, say you have a 2 oz bottle of lotion that you sell as a travel size. Then you decide to hand them out as free samples at a fair or show. Because you sell a product that is the SAME as the free sample, the samples must have met all the cosmetic labeling requirements. However, if you decide to hand out a 1 oz sample and don't otherwise sell the product packaged that way, then you could just put "Free Sample" on the package and don't have to meet all cosmetic labeling requirements.

Package

The term "package" is defined several ways in different places, but the general concept is that a "package" is:

> *A container or wrapping, other than a shipping container or wrapping, in which a consumer commodity is delivered or displayed to retail purchasers.*

The package is the outer container of a product; the part that the consumer sees. If the product doesn't have an outer container, then the immediate container (the bottle or jar, for example) is the package.

If your hand lotion is in a box, then the box is the "package". If the lotion is displayed in the bottle, then the bottle is the "package". If the lotion is displayed in a clear box and the only labeling is on the bottle (which must be able to be easily read), then the "package" is the bottle.

Additional Definition for Package

The Uniform Packaging and Labeling Regulation (UPLR) defines a package as:

> *Any commodity that is enclosed in a container or wrapped in any manner in advance of wholesale or retail sale; OR*

> *Any commodity whose weight or measure has been determined in advance of wholesale or retail sale.*

In this case, if the commodity or product is somehow contained, enclosed or wrapped **OR** if the weight is determined before it is sold by wholesale or retail, then that is the package.

"Naked" (unwrapped) soaps sold by the bar are considered to be packaged if the weight is determined beforehand. However, unwrapped soaps that are displayed for sale may qualify for off-package retail labeling (see Chapter 10).

Case Packs / Wholesale Boxes

The box or container used to hold a case of items is also considered a package for labeling purposes.

If you normally package and sell your products in case packs (whether wholesale or retail), then the outside of the case requires labeling in accordance with the Fair Packaging and Labeling Act and/or the state version of the Uniform Packaging and Labeling laws and must state the product, manufacturer and net contents.

In that example, the outside box holding several naked soaps is the package.

Inner or Immediate Container

The inner or immediate container is the one that actually contains the product. It would be the bottle, jar, bag or tin, for example.

It is usually referred to as the "inner container" when it is enclosed in a "package" (see above). When not held in an outer package, then it is typically referred to as the "immediate container".

Label

The term "label" has several different definitions; some from the actual regulations and some from the way the regulations are applied.

In some cases there is a distinction between the "label" and the "labeling" (see below).

Fair Product Labeling Act

"Label" is defined under the FPLA as:

> *The written, printed or graphic matter affixed to any consumer commodity or affixed to or appearing upon a package containing any consumer commodity.*

In this case, the label is not only what is on the inner or immediate container or product, it is also what is on any package containing a consumer commodity. It would apply to what is on both the jar of hand cream AND the box the jar is enclosed in AND the case pack holding the items.

Food, Drug & Cosmetic Act

"Label" is defined under the FD&C Act as:

> *A display of written, printed or graphic matter upon the immediate container.*

By this definition, it is the information attached to the container that actually holds the product. In other words, the printed band wrapped around the soap or the printed label stuck on a bottle or jar.

However, the FD&C Act requires that any information that must appear on the immediate container ALSO appear on the outside container of a retail package (or be visible and legible though it).

Uniform Packaging and Labeling Regulation

The Uniform Packaging and Labeling Regulation defines the "label" as:

> *Any written, printed, or graphic matter affixed to, applied to, attached to, blown into, formed, molded into, embossed on, or appearing upon or adjacent to a consumer commodity or a package containing any consumer commodity, for purposes of branding, identifying, or giving any information with respect to the commodity or to the contents of the package, except that an inspector's tag or other nonpromotional matter affixed to or appearing upon a consumer commodity shall not be considered a label requiring the repetition of label information required by this regulation.*

Labeling

The FD&C Act considers that "labeling" is not just what's on the box or bottle. It is:

*All labels and other written, printed or graphic material **on or accompanying** a product in interstate commerce or held for sale.*

It includes labels, inserts, risers, display packs, leaflets, promotional literature or any other printed information distributed with a product.

As mentioned earlier, when the FDA seeks to determine whether a product has been misbranded or is being promoted as a drug, not a cosmetic, they look at all the information on and around the product, including promotional materials and statements made on the selling website.

Labels and Labeling

From the above definitions of "label" and "labeling" it can be seen that just about any type of information that goes on or is attached to the package or accompanying the product in any way is considered to be part of the label/labeling information being provided to the consumer. As such all of it is subject to the scrutiny of the governing bodies for determining regulatory compliance.

Principal Display Panel (PDP)

The PDP is defined as:

The part of a label that the consumer sees or examines when a product is displayed for retail sale.

Usually it is the front panel of the package or container. It's what the consumer sees as they walk by or what they would be most likely to read first when picking up and inspecting the product.

If the product container is inside a box or other type of package, only the outer package has a PDP.

The size of the PDP determines the minimum text size that may be used for specific elements on the label.

Calculating PDP Size

For the purposes of calculating the PDP size, it is the size of the whole surface area bearing the PDP.

In other words, if you have a large box but elect to put a very small label on it, the PDP size (and the required text size) is determined by the box, not by the size of the label stuck on it.

Cylindrical Container

For the PDP of a cylindrical container, the PDP size is 40% of the entire surface.

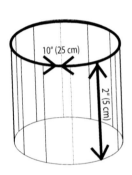

It is calculated by multiplying the height times the circumference and then taking 40% of that space.

Using the example here, the forumula to calculate the PDP would be a two step process:

First: **10" x 2" = 20 sq in**

and then: **20 sq in x .40 = 8 sq. in.**

OR

First: **5cm x 25cm = 125 sq cm**

and then: **125 x .40 = 50 sq. cm**

Rectangular Container

For a rectangular package, the PDP size is equal to one entire side of the rectangle.

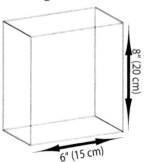

The actual amount of space is calculated as height x width.

Using the example here, the PDP would be:

8" x 6" = 48 sq. inches   OR

20 cm x 15 cm = 300 sq. cm

Other Shaped Container PDP

For any other shaped container, the PDP is calculated as 40% of the total surface of the container (excluding top, bottom, shoulder and flanges), unless the container has an obvious principal display panel.

Other Shaped Container Examples

Example A: For foil bag, like a coffee bag, that is 8" tall and 5" wide, the total surface of the container would be 40% surface area of the front and back:

$$[(8" \times 5") \times 2] \times 40\% = 32 \text{ sq. inches}$$

Example B: A low, flat jar with very little available space on the sides but a large top, and where the top is generally what is presented to the consumer. The top would be the principal display panel.

Very small containers

For a very small container (like a small perfume bottle or other decorative container) or one that holds less than 1/4 ounce (by weight) or 1/8 fluid ounce, the principal display panel would be a tear-away tag or tape attached to the container or the display panel of a card to which the product is affixed. In some cases very small containers qualify for off-package labeling (see Chapter 10).

PDP Summary

Package Shape	PDP Calculation
Rectangular	One entire side
Cylindrical	40% of height x circumference
Any other shape	40% of total container surface, excluding top, bottom, shoulder & flanges
Decorative container; or holds less than 1/4 ounce (by weight) or 1/8 fluid ounce.	Tear-away tag or tape attached to container or display panel of a card to which the product is affixed.

Informational Panels

The Informational Panels of a package or immediate container consist of all the areas that are NOT part of the Principal Display Panel. This is usually the back and sides of the package and/or product and sometimes the bottom and/or top.

As stated above, if the product container is inside a package, only the outer container has a PDP. Therefore, all the panels on the immediate container are informational if it is inside another package.

For example, for a lotion bottle in a box, the BOX has the principal display panel. All panels on the box that are not part of the PDP are informational panels. All panels on the BOTTLE are informational panels.

Chapter 4
General Rules for Product Labels

There are some label requirements that are universal, regardless of what type product it is. The FDA's Food, Drug and Cosmetic Act, the FTC's Fair Product Labeling Act and the Universal Weighs and Measures Law are all written similarly when it comes to the basic labeling requirements.

Comparable basic regulations have also been adopted by Canada and the EU and probably other countries. There is an on-going international effort to coordinate cosmetic labeling laws.

Display of Information

The information must be on a panel that is normally presented or displayed under typical circumstances. The information shouldn't be placed on the bottom panel unless the package is very small and is normally picked up to be inspected for possible purchase.

Panel Size

The panel must be large enough to provide sufficient space to prominently display the required information. In other words, you can't put a tiny label on a big box and expect to use tiny text on the label.

Clarity of Information

The information must be clear and able to be read by a typical consumer under normal conditions.

Background Contrast

There must be sufficient contrast between the background and the text so that the information on the label is conspicuous and readable.

No Obscuring Designs or Images

The required statements must not be obscured or crowded by designs, images, clip art or other pictures or printed matter.

Language

English Language Statements

All labeling information that is required by law or regulation must be in English. The only exception is if the product will be distributed only in a U.S. territory where a different language is predominant, such as Puerto Rico.

Foreign Language Statements

If the label or labeling contains any statements in a foreign language, then all label information required under the FD&C Act must appear in that language in addition to English.

Type Size

Each different part of the label has specific type size requirements. (Covered later in the section for each part of the label).

Since different type fonts have different size capital and lowercase letters, the determining size is based on the actual measurement of the letter sizes, not the font size.

If only upper case or capital letters are used, an upper case "L" is used to determine the text size.

If both upper and lower case or just lower case letters are used, then the size of the text is determined by the height of the lower case letter "o".

Example Type Sizes

Comparing sizes of Arial, Times New Roman & Bodoni MT Condensed using Uppercase "L" for all uppercase words and lowercase "o" for upper and lower case words

All Upper Case

1/32 "

L ARIAL 3 pt
L TIMES NEW ROMAN 3 pt
L BODONI MT CONDENSED 4pt

1/16 "

L ARIAL 6 pt

L TIMES 6 point

L BODONI MT CONDENSED 8.5pt

1/8 "

L ARIAL 12 pt

L TIMES 12 point

L BODONI MT CONDENSED 14pt

3/16 "

L ARIAL 18 pt

L TIMES 19 pt

L BODONI COND 20pt

Upper and Lower Case

1/32 "

o Arial 5 pt
o Times New Roman 5 pt
o Bodoni 6 pt

1/16 "

o Arial 9 pt
o Times New Roman 10 point
o Bodoni 12 pt

1/8 "

o Arial 16 pt
o Times 18 pt
o Bodoni 20 pt

3/16 "

o Arial 24 pt
o Times 28
o Bodoni 30 pt

Regardless of the approved type size, the text must above all be readable. The quality of printing may be a factor in the readability of very small text sizes as it requires high-resolution printing to make very small text readable.

Even if 1/16" or 1/32" text size is acceptable by the regulations, if the label is printed by a printer with insufficient resolution to render the text clearly, then it is a violation and the product is misbranded.

Required on the Outer Container or Package

Principal Display Panel

- a) Name of the Product
- b) Identity of Product
- c) Unsubstantiated Safety Warning (if required)
- d) Net Quantity of Contents

Information Panels

- a) Directions for Safe Use
- b) Warnings (if required)
- c) Name and Place of Business
- d) Ingredient Declaration
- e) Any Other Required Information

Name & Identity of the Product

The Principal Display Panel (and the Front Panel of the inner or immediate container, if there is one) must display the name and identity of the product.

The name is generally the brand name for the product, typically read as an adjective on the label, i.e. "MyBrand™ Body Lotion" or "MyBrand™ Longlasting Mascara".

The identity is what the product is or does and the way it is presented must clearly communicate that to the consumer.

The identity may be in the form of the common or usual name of the product, i.e. "body lotion" or "MyBrand Body Lotion") It may be in the form of a descriptive name or a fanciful name, so long as it is clear what the product is. It may even be in the form of an illustration, i.e. a bathtub full of bubbles for bubble bath.

The identity of the product must be in bold type and in a size reasonably related to the most prominent printed matter (which is

---

Required on the Inner (Immediate) Container

If the product is packaged and displayed in a non-transparent outer package (such as a box or folding carton) then the inner (immediate) container must contain the following information.

Front Panel

    a) Name & Identity of the Product

Information Panels

    a) Directions for Safe Use

    b) Warnings (if required)

    c) Name and Place of Business

    d) Quantity of Contents

    e) Any Other Required Information

Note: If the outer container is removed and the product may be displayed for sale without it, then the label of the immediate container becomes a label of an outer container and must meet the appropriate labeling requirements for an outer container label.

---

usually the name of the product) and must be in line and generally parallel to the base on on which the product rests when displayed at retail.

Using an Ingredient in the Name

According to the specific FDA regulation on what constitutes misbranding of a cosmetic (Title 21, Part 701.1 Misbranding),

> **A product is misbranded if the name or identity of the product includes the name of one ingredient but not all ingredients.**

In other words, a lotion named "Shea Butter Lotion" is misbranded if it contains more that just shea butter.

Taking it one step further, if a qualifying statement about one or more ingredients after the name looks like it's actually part of the name, that could also be interpreted to be misbranding. For example, if your label stated "MyBrand™ Body Lotion with Shea

Butter" and it could reasonably be read that the name of the product is "Body Lotion with Shea Butter", then the shea butter is included in the name and it is misbranded.

Going to the store you will find many products by companies large and small that include the name of an ingredient in the name or identity of the product. Regardless of what others are doing, your product is misbranded if the name or identity includes one ingredient and excludes others[1].

Unsubstantiated Safety Warning

If an unsubstantiated safety warning is required, it must be at least 1/16" high and clearly stated on the PDP. (See Chapter 11 for details)

Name and Place of Business

The name and place of business must be included on informational panels for both the outer package and the immediate container (if any). (See Chapter 5 for details.)

Net Quantity of Contents

A clear statement of the net contents of the product must be included on the principal display panel of the outer package and on an informational panel of the immediate container (if any). The size of text used for the net contents is determined by the size of the principal display panel. (See Chapter 6 for details.)

Directions for Safe Use

Any necessary text to explain how to safely use the product is required on informational panels on the outer package and the immediate container (if any).

---

1 The author had a detailed email exchange and a long phone conversation with an FDA representative in the Cosmetic Compliance Division about this. His comment was that "it happens all the time" but they don't have the manpower to enforce that part of the regulations. He was very clear, however, that it is still misbranding under the law, even though they don't generally enforce it.

The directions must be sufficient so the consumer understands how to use the product and can make an informed decision on whether or not to purchase it.

Warnings

Any warnings required must be:

a) prominent and conspicuous, so it is likely to be read by ordinary consumers at the time of purchase

b) printed in bold type on a contrasting background

c) at least 1/16" in height

The "Unsubstantiated Safety Warning" has additional requirements. (See Chapter 11 for details.)

Ingredient Declaration

Last, but certainly not least, all consumer cosmetic products require a complete declaration of all ingredients listed on an informational panel of the outer package. (See Chapters 7 - 10 for details on the requirements of the ingredient declaration.)

Chapter 5
Business Name & Address

The business name and address of the person or business responsible for the product must be on every consumer cosmetic and commodity. It is required on an informational panel on both the outer package and the inner (immediate) container (if any). It should not be placed on the principal display panel.

The name and business address appearing on the label may be those of the manufacturer, packer or distributor. If the actual manufacturer is not named, then the name listed must be preceded by a phrase such as "Manufactured for ...", "Distributed by ...", or other appropriate wording.

The name of the firm must be the corporate name or official business name. An individual or sole proprietorship should use the "doing business as" name, if one exists and is registered with the appropriate state agency. If there is no DBA, then the personal name must be used on the label. Stating the name of a corporation's particular division is optional.

The address should be the principal place of business. The business address must include the street address, city, state, and the ZIP code.

The street address may be omitted if the business is listed in a current city or telephone directory under the business name or DBA used on the label. Even if the street address is omitted, the city, state and zip code must still be listed.

The phone number, email and website address are not required, but may be included on the label.

Chapter 6
Quantity of Contents

All packaging and labeling regulations, whether they are from the FTC, FDA, EPA or under the Uniform Weights and Measures Laws, very strictly require that every package include a declaration of the quantity of contents. It must state the net quantity of the actual product in the package (measured without any packaging included).

Use of the Term "Net"

The wording required by the various regulations differs slightly, but the intent is to ensure that the consumer knows what the measurement means so he/she can accurately compare products and determine their relative value.

Wording for Weight

For cosmetic items packaged by weight, the FDA requires the term "net weight" or "net wt" be used.

For non-cosmetic consumer commodities that are packaged by weight, the Uniform Weights and Meausres Law recommends and the Fair Packaging and Labeling Act requires that the weight declaration is stated as "net weight," "net wt" or "net mass" or may stand alone.

In both cases, the words may come before or after the actual numerical weight.

Wording for Liquid Volume

For liquid products, all regulations state that the terms "net contents", "net" or nothing may be used.

Generally the liquid volume statement comes after the numeric statement.

Metric Measurements

The use of metric measurements is required by the Fair Packaging and Labeling Act for consumer commodities and recommended by the Uniform Weights and Measures Laws, but not required on cosmetics regulated by the Food, Drug and Cosmetic Act.

However, since most cosmetics are transported and sold in states where some version of the UWML have been enacted, it is becoming standard practice to include the metric measurements on cosmetics.

Placement

The net contents statement must appear:

a) within the bottom 30% of the Primary Display Panel of the outer container, generally parallel to and in line with the base on which the package rests, and

b) on an information panel of the inner container (if the outer container isn't also the immediate container).

If the cosmetic is sold in the immediate container, then the net contents must display within the bottom 30% of the PDP of the immediate container, generally parallel to and in line with the base on which the container rests.

The "bottom location" requirement is waived for PDPs of 5 square inches or less.

Prominent & Conspicuous

The declaration of the quantity of contents must:

a) be a distinct item, separated from other printed matter by a space at least equal to the height of the lettering used in the declaration and twice the width of the letter "N"

b) be easily legible

c) display in bold face type

d) distinctly contrast with the background

e) have an aspect ratio of height to width that does not exceed 3:1 (the letters can't be more than 3 times taller than they are wide)

f) be of the required type size, based on the size of the PDP:

PDP area less than 5 sq. in.	1/16" type
PDP area 5 - 25 sq. in.	1/8" type
PDP area 25 - 100 sq. in.	3/16" type

Small Containers

Cosmetics in packages containing less than 1/4 avoirdupois ounce (by weight) or 1/8 fluid ounce are exempt from having the net quantity of contents declaration on the immediate container if it is affixed to a properly labeled display card or packaged in an outer container for retail sale.

Qualifying Statements

The quantity of contents may not, under any circumstances, be qualified by the addition of the words:

"when packed"   "minimum"
"not less than" "approximately"

or any similar qualifying statement.

Accuracy

The net quantity of contents declaration must accurately state the amount of product that is actually in the container, without counting any part of the container or package. It must be stated in terms of weight, volume, measure, numerical count, or a combination of count with the weight, volume or measure.

Reasonable variations due to loss or gain of moisture or deviations in good manufacturing practice are acceptable, but in no case may the quantity of contents be overstated.

Soap

Soap typically gradually looses weight as it ages, due to the evaporation of the water content. Typically, the older the bar of soap, the lighter it becomes.

It is the responsibility of the labeler to accurately calculate the net contents of a bar of soap as the least amount it could be when sold. The quantity of contents declaration on a bar of soap must not be stated as "approx. 4 oz" or "not less than 4 oz".

For "true soap" (made with lye and oils) calculating the weight of the ingredients in the soap less the water content will give the weight of the soap with all water evaporated out; the least possible weight of the soap.

Rounding

When showing the conversion between the inch/pound measurement and the metric measurement, the number can be rounded to avoid having more than three decimal places in the number.

Make sure when you convert and round the amount that you do not exaggerate nor sacrifice accuracy. NEVER overstate the net contents; round down if necessary,

See Appendix D for guidelines and examples of rounding.

Metric Measurements

The metric standard to use is the International System of Units (SI) as established in 1960. It is referred to as SI, as in "the SI declaration" or the "SI Unit".

SI Unit to Use

The SI declaration should be the largest whole unit with the remainder shown as a decimal fraction.

The SI declaration should result in a number between 1 - 1000, and be shown in three digits (except where the quantity is below 100 grams, milliliters, centimeters, square centimeters or cubic centimeters, where it can be shown in two digits). In any case, any final zero appearing to the right of the decimal point need not be displayed.

Correct	*Incorrect*
500 g	0.5 kg
1.96 kg	1960 g
750 mL	0.75 L
750 mm or 75 cm	0.75 m

Metric Abbreviations & Symbols			
centimeter	cm	cubic meter	m^3
cubic centimeter	cm^3	kilogram	kg
meter	m	gram	g
milligram	mg	millimeter	mm
liter	L or l	square meter	m^2
milliliter	mL or ml	cubic decimeter	dm^3
square centimeter	cm^2	square decimeter	dm^2
Only the above unit abbreviations and symbols may be used in a metric quantity statement on a package.			

Symbols are always written in the singular form.

SI Units (except for Liter) are not capitalized. Periods are not used. Only decimal fractions are used with SI Units.

The SI declaration may be placed either before or after the inch/pound declaration.   In most cases having only the SI declaration without the inch/pound version is not allowed.

Inch/Pound Measurements

Inch/Pound measurements are those with which most Americans are familiar (inch, foot, yard, ounce, pound, etc).

Since "ounce" can be used for fluid or solid measurements, when used as a fluid measurement it should be stated as "fl oz" unless the proper meaning is already clear by association of terms (i.e. "1 pint, 4 ounces").

With Inch/Pound symbols, periods should not be used although it is not incorrect to do so. Both upper and lower case letters are acceptable. Both regular and decimal fractions may be used with Inch/Pound Units.

Inch/Pound Abbreviations & Symbols			
avoirdupois	avdp	ounce	oz
piece	pc	count	ct
pint	pt	cubic	cu
pound	lb	each	ea
feet or foot	ft	quart	qt
fluid	fl	square	sq
gallon	gal	weight	wt
inch	in	yard	yd
liquid	liq	drained	dr
diameter	dia		

Only the above unit abbreviations and symbols may be used in an inch/pound quantity statement on a package.

Symbols are always written in the singular form, i.e. "3 gal" not "3 gals.".

Liquid Products

If the product is liquid, the measurement must be in terms of fluid measure. Fluid measures must express the volume of the fluid at 68°F (20°C).

Inch/Pound Fluid Units

In the Inch/Pound system, fluid measure is stated in terms of fluid ounce, pint, quart and gallon.

If the quantity is less than 1 pint, it should be stated in fluid ounces and fractions thereof.

If the quantity is more than a pint, but less than 1 gallon, it must be stated in the largest whole unit with the remainder stated as fractions of the whole unit or the next smaller unit(s).

If the quantity is more than 1 gallon, then it should be stated in gallons, then fractions of gallons or the next smaller unit.

Additionally, the FDA requires that the declaration on cosmetics also be in the total number of ounces. While shown in all the examples following, the total number of ounces could be omitted from a consumer commodity not regulated by the FDA.

Metric (SI) Fluid Units

Fluid measure in the metric system is milliliter and Liter.

If the quantity is less than 1 Liter, it should be expressed in milliliters.

If the quantity is more than 1 Liter, it should be expressed in liters and decimal fractions to not more than three places.

Correct Liquid Content Statement - Example 1

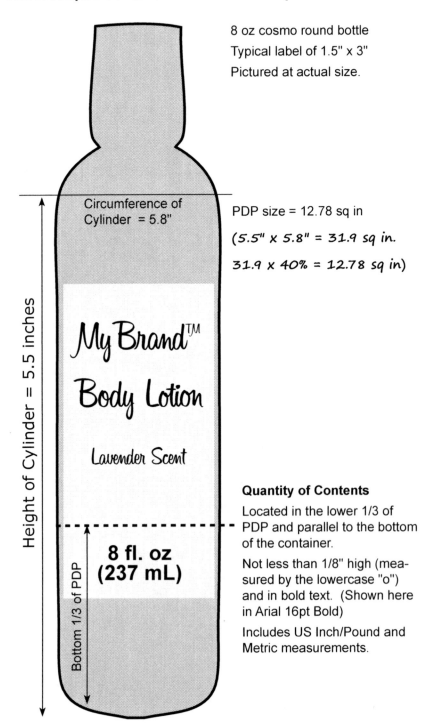

8 oz cosmo round bottle
Typical label of 1.5" x 3"
Pictured at actual size.

Circumference of Cylinder = 5.8"

PDP size = 12.78 sq in

(5.5" x 5.8" = 31.9 sq in.

31.9 x 40% = 12.78 sq in)

Height of Cylinder = 5.5 inches

My Brand™

Body Lotion

Lavender Scent

Bottom 1/3 of PDP

**8 fl. oz
(237 mL)**

Quantity of Contents

Located in the lower 1/3 of PDP and parallel to the bottom of the container.

Not less than 1/8" high (measured by the lowercase "o") and in bold text. (Shown here in Arial 16pt Bold)

Includes US Inch/Pound and Metric measurements.

Correct Liquid Content Statement - *Example 2*

4 oz boston round bottle
Typical label of 1.5" x 2"
Pictured at actual size.

PDP size = 4.8 sq in

(3" x 6" = 12 sq in.

12 x 40% = 4.8 sq in)

Quantity of Contents

Located in the lower 1/3 of PDP and parallel to the bottom of the container.

Not less than 1/16" high (measured by the lowercase "o") and in bold text. (Shown here in Arial 9 pt Bold)

Includes US Inch/Pound and Metric measurements.

Correct Liquid Content Statement - *Example 3*

Gallon jug
Typical label of 4" x 5"
Pictured at about half size.

PDP size = 52.5 sq in

(7" x 18.75" = 131.25 sq in.

131.25 x 40% = 52.5 sq in)

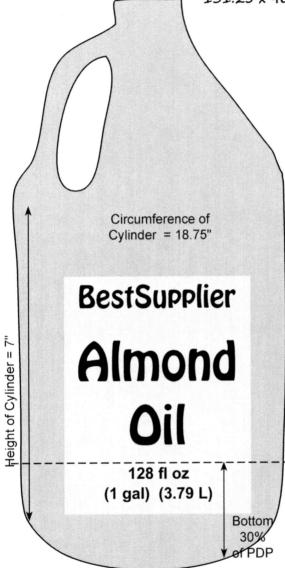

Circumference of
Cylinder = 18.75"

Height of Cylinder = 7"

BestSupplier

Almond Oil

**128 fl oz
(1 gal) (3.79 L)**

Bottom
30%
of PDP

Quantity of Contents

Located in the lower 1/3 of PDP and parallel to the bottom of the container.

Not less than 3/16" high (measured by the lowercase "o") and in bold text. (shown here in Arial 12 pt Bold to be in proportion with this half-size image; on the actual label it would need to be about 24 pt Bold).

Includes US Inch/ Pound and Metric measurements.

Additional Correct Examples of Net Content Statements for Liquid Products

1/8 oz.

Net 1/8 fl oz (3.7 mL)
3.7 mL (0.12 fl oz)
Net contents 0.12 fl oz (3.7 mL)

4 oz.

Net contents 4 fl oz (119 mL)
Net 4 fl oz (119 mL)
4 fl oz (119 mL)
119 mL (4 fl oz)

24 oz. Cosmetic:

24 fl. oz. (1.5 pt) (710 mL)
24 fl oz (1 pt 8 fl oz) (710 mL)

24 oz Consumer Commodity:

1.5 pt (710 mL) (24 fl oz)
1.5 pt (24 fl oz) (710 mL)

56 oz. Cosmetic:

56 fl. oz. (1 qt. 1.5 pt) (1.66 L)
56 fl oz. (1 qt. 1 pt. 8 fl oz) (1.66 L)
56 fl oz. (1 qt 1-1/2 pt) (1.66 L)
56 fl oz. (1 qt. 1.5 pt) (1.66 L)
56 fl oz. (1-3/4 qt) (1.66 L)

56 oz. Consumer Commodity:

1 qt 1 pt. 8 fl oz   (1.66 L)
1 qt 1-1/2 pt   (1.66 L)
1.66 L (1 qt 1.5 pt)
1.66 qt (56 oz) (1.66 L)
1 qt 1.5 pt (56 fl oz) (166 L)

Note that for products that are more than 1 pint, the cosmetic labeling requirements differ from the requirements for a non-cosmetic consumer commodity.

Solid, Semi-Solid or Viscous Products

If the product is solid, semi-solid, viscous or a mixture of solid and liquid it should be measured in terms of weight.

For cosmetic products the term "net weight" or "net wt" must be used in conjunction with a weight statement. For non-cosmetic products the term "net mass" may be used instead. It is not acceptable to leave the "net" statement off.

Inch/Pound Weight/Mass Units

In the Inch/Pound system, weight is expressed in terms of avoir-dupois (weight) pounds and ounces.

If the weight is less than one pound, it should be stated in terms of ounces.

If the weight is more than one pound, then the weight should be stated in pounds and ounces or pounds and fractions of pounds.

Metric (SI) Weight Units

In the metric system, weight measure is in terms of milligrams, grams, and kilograms.

It should be expressed in the largest whole unit with the remainder expressed in decimal points.

If the quantity is more than 1 pound, but less than 4 pounds, the weight is stated first in the total ounces and then in the largest unit and fractions thereof. Metrics are optional according to the FDA, but included in these examples as they are generally required by state law.

Additionally, the FDA requires that the declaration on cosmetics also be in the total number of ounces. While shown in all the examples following, the total number of ounces could be omitted from a consumer commodity not regulated by the FDA.

Correct Weight Content Statement - Example 1

2" x 3" bars of soap, shown full size.   PDP is 6 square inches.

Quantity of Contents

Located in the lower 1/3 of PDP and parallel to the bottom.

Not less than 1/8" high (measured by the lowercase "o") and in bold text. (Shown here in Arial 12 pt Bold)

Includes US Inch/Pound and Metric measurements.

Correct Weight Content Statement - Example 2

16 oz Jar (89/400 lid size)
Typical label of 2.25" x 2.5"
Pictured at actual size.

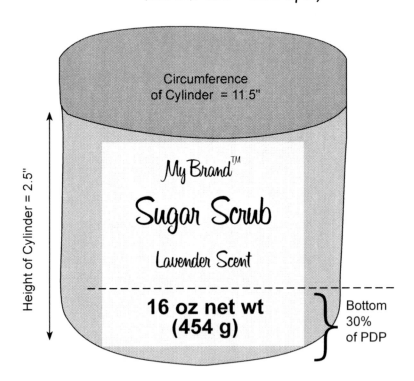

Principal Display Panel size = 11.5 sq in

(11.5" x 2.5" = 28.75 sq in.

28.75 x 40% = 11.5 sq in)

Circumference
of Cylinder = 11.5"

Height of Cylinder = 2.5"

My Brand™

Sugar Scrub

Lavender Scent

16 oz net wt
(454 g)

Bottom
30%
of PDP

Quantity of Contents

Located in the lower 1/3 of PDP and parallel to the bottom.

Not less than 1/8" high (measured by the lowercase "o") and in bold text. (Shown here in Arial 16 pt Bold)

Includes US Inch/Pound and Metric measurements.

Correct Weight Content Statement - Example 3

Talc Shaker (5" x 1 7/8" diameter)
Pictured at actual size.

PDP size = 12 sq in

(5" x 6" = 30 sq in

30 x 40% = 12 sq in)

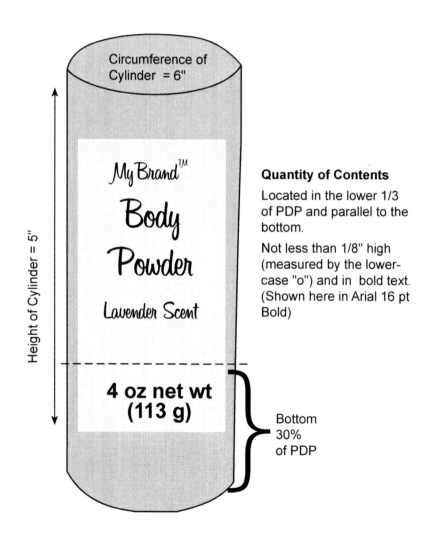

Circumference of
Cylinder = 6"

Height of Cylinder = 5"

My Brand™

Body

Powder

Lavender Scent

4 oz net wt
(113 g)

Quantity of Contents

Located in the lower 1/3
of PDP and parallel to the
bottom.

Not less than 1/8" high
(measured by the lower-
case "o") and in bold text.
(Shown here in Arial 16 pt
Bold)

Bottom
30%
of PDP

Additional Correct Examples of Net Content Statements for Solid, Semi-Soli or Viscous Products

1/8 oz.

Net 1/8 oz (3.6g)
3.6 g (0.12 oz)
Net weight 3.6 g (0.12 oz)

4 oz.

Net contents 4 oz (114 g)
Net 4 oz (114 g)
4 oz (114 g) net wt
113 g (4 oz)

40 oz. Cosmetic:

40 oz. (2.5 lb) (1.34 kg)
40 oz. (2 lb 8 oz) (1.34 kg)
40 oz. (2 - 1/2 lb) (1.34 kg)

40 oz. Consumer Commodity:

2.5 lb (1.34 kg)
2 lb 8 oz (1.34 kg)
1.34 kg (2.5 lb)
1.34 kg (2 lb 8 oz)

Note that for products that are more than 1 pound, the cosmetic labeling requirements differ from the requirements for a consumer commodity.

Multi-Unit Packages[1]

A multi-unit package contains more than one of the *same item*, i.e. a case pack or cosmetic compact.

Packaged Individual Units

If the inside units are packaged for retail sale, then the outside package must state:

a) number of individual units

b) quantity of each individual unit

c) total quantity of contents of the multi-unit package

Note that this applies to case packs. If you package 12 soaps in a box or 6 lotions in a package as your wholesale case, then the outside of the case pack must have the required quantity of contents statements (as above).

Correct Examples - Multi-Unit Package (packaged units)

> **12 soap bars**
> **Net Wt 113 g (4 oz) each**

> **6 bottles**
> **8 fl oz (237 mL) each**

> **4 eye shadows**
> **Net Wt 1/8 oz (3.6 g) each**

---

[1] The term "multi-unit package" is defined and used differently for the quantity of contents declaration guidelines than it is for the ingredients statement.

Unpackaged Individual Units

When a multi-unit package contains unlabeled individual units which are not intended for individual retail sale, only a statement of the total contents is required. Stating the number of individual units is optional.

Correct Examples - Multi-Unit Package (unpackaged units)

Total Net Wt 1.36 kg (3 lb)

12 soap bars **Total Net Wt 1.36 kg (3 lb)**

12 soap bars **Net Wt 113 g (4 oz) each**

All three examples are acceptable ways to label the same multi-unit container of unpackaged indivudal units.

Bathroom tissue - 8 rolls **440 sq ft (40.92 sq m) total area**

Bathroom tissue - 8 rolls **440 sq ft (40.92 sq m) total area** **Each roll 440 two-ply sheets** **4.5 in x 4.0 in (11.4 cm x 10.2 cm)**

Both examples are acceptable ways to label the same multi-unit container of unpackaged indivudal units.

Variety Package

A variety package is one that is intended for retail sale and contains two or more packages or units of similar but different items. Gift sets and gift packages are typical examples of a variety package.

The quantity of contents declaration on a variety package must be stated as:

a) The number of units for each identical item followed by the measure of that item.

b) The total quantity by weight or mass, volume, measure, and count, as appropriate of the whole package. The statement of total quantity must appear as the last item and can't be more prominent than the other information.

Items that differ only in weight or mass, measure volume, appearance, or quality are considered similar (but not identical) so must be labeled separately. For example, two lotions with different fragrances would be considered similar but not identical and must the listed on the outside package individually.

Correct Examples - Variety Package

```
2 soap bars net wt 3.2 oz (90 g) each
   1 soap bar net wt 5.0 oz (141 g)
```

```
   1 jar cream net wt 4 oz (114 g)
 1 jar bath salts net wt 16 oz (454 g)
  Total 2 jars net wt 20 oz (568 g)
```

Supplementary Quantity Declarations

In certain cases additional quantity information may be placed on the PDP with the intent of giving the consumer additional information.

Candles

Candles traditionally have the amount of burn time stated as an additional measurement for the candle.

"Economy Size" or "Budget Size"

You may say that the package is "Economy Size" if you offer at least one other package of the same brand/product AND the unit price of the large one is at least 5% less than the other.

Example: You have a shampoo that comes in two sizes, 8 oz and 24 oz. The 8 oz bottle sells for $12.00, or $1.50 per oz. 5% less per unit (ounce) would be $1.425 per oz or $34.20 for a 24 oz bottle. Therefore, the 24 oz size could be labeled "Economy Size" if it is priced less than $34.20.

Number of Applications (Cosmetics)

If there is a numerical count or other way to measure the weight or size of individual units within the package, it may also be placed with the Quantity of Contents declaration. If stated, it must go on the PDP along with the total weight statement.

Example - Number of Applications

For a set of bath teas, 4 tea bags in the package, each tea bag containing 1 oz of herbs.

> **Net Wt 4 oz (114 g)**
> **4 applications**

Cosmetic Kits

If a package contains all the parts necessary to make up a single whole that is delivered as an application, the net contents may be stated in terms of the number of applications as per the instructions.

Example - Net Weight Statement for a Kit

You sell a facial mask kit that comes with a jar of dry ingredients, a bottle of liquid ingredients and a bottle of essential oil. The directions tell how much of each part of the kit should be mixed to make one application and there is enough of each ingredient to make 3 applications in all.

The front panel label quantity of contents should read:

3 applications

Numerical Count

A numerical count of the items may also go on the quantity of contents declaration on the PDP.

Example - Numerical Count

You sell a package of 6 bath bombs, each one weighing 1 oz. for a total weight of 6 oz.

The front panel label quantity of contents should read:

6 bath bombs
Net Wt 171 g (6 oz)

Informational Panel

If you want, you can add one or more supplemental declarations of weight, measure or count on an informational panel (not the primary display panel). Any supplemental statement must not include a qualifier that tends to exaggerate the amount of commodity contained in the package.

For example, on a jar of bath salts you would put the actual weight on the PDP, but could add "Enough for 5 baths" on an informational panel.

Some products have traditional measurement units that the consumer expects to find on the label.

Chapter 7
The
Ingredient Declaration

This chapter explains the details on how to put together an ingredient listing; what needs to go on it, what order it should go in and where it must be placed. The three following chapters cover special circumstances in writing the ingredient listing.

However, there are a few myths about the ingredient listing that we need to dispel before going forward.

Myths About the Ingredient List

Myth #1 - If you put an ingredient list on a package of soap, that causes it to qualify as a cosmetic.

A soap (as per the definitions covered in Chapter 2) only becomes a cosmetic IF there is a cosmetic claim made for the product. Putting the ingredients on the package does not make it a cosmetic (unless cosmetic claims are made in the ingredient list).

Myth #2 - The ingredients always and only go in descending order of prominence (most to least).

Listing the ingredients in descending order of prominence is acceptable in all cases and is never wrong. However, there are some exceptions and alternatives that make the ingredient listing much easier, particularly where color additives are involved or where you have several items packaged together.

Myth #3 - The ingredient list must go on the actual product container.

Actually, the ingredient list must go on the outer package. If the jar or bottle is the outer package, then yes, it goes on the jar or container. But if the outer container is a box, bag, carton or something similar, then the ingredient listing goes there and isn't required on the product container.

Myth #4 - When one ingredient is made up of other ingredients it can be listed with "(and) ".

No. Each ingredient must be listed in the order of predominance, even if it was added to the mix as part of something else. For example, if you add a preservative blend, each individual ingredient in the preservative blend must be listed individually according to its percentage in the entire formulation.

Those are the myths - now on to the truths in the details.

When is an Ingredient Listing Required?

An ingredient listing is **required** on cosmetics that are:

a) customarily sold at retail; or

b) used in the performance of services conducted within the household.

An ingredient listing is **not required** on:

a) consumer items that are not cosmetics;

b) cosmetic products to be used in professional establishments by professionals;

c) free samples of cosmetic products; or

d) soaps that make no cosmetic claims.

Remember, though, that if a free sample is the same as a product normally sold at retail then the ingredient listing is required, even if the product is also labeled "for professional use only" or "free sample."

Ingredient Listing

Required

» A hand lotion sold at a retail craft fair

» "Moisturizing Soap" sold wholesale to a gift store

» Tanning oil for use at home

» Small bottle of shampoo given out as a "free sample" but also sold as a "travel size"

» A jar of bath salts

» A set of mineral makeup

» Massage Oil

Not Required

» Shampoo sold only to beauty salons for use by professionals (and not resold by them)

» Free hotel guest room amenities

» Free lotion samples (not sold otherwise)

» Soap (lye and oil soap) labeled as "soap" with no cosmetic claims

» Dish washing or laundry soap (not cosmetic)

» Drawer sachet (not cosmetic)

» Candle (not a cosmetic)

Location of the Ingredient List

The ingredient listing is only required on an information panel on the label of the outer container. The ingredient listing should not be placed on the PDP.

If the product is packaged in an outer box or carton, the ingredient label is only required on the outside box or carton, not on the inside product container. You can still put the ingredient listing on the immediate container if you want, but you don't have to.

If there is no outer packaging (or if the outer packaging is clear) then the ingredient label must go on the immediate container (which, in this case, is also the outer container).

Ingredient List Visibility

The ingredient list must be easily visible and able to be read and understood by an average person.

Large Enough Type

Generally, the type size must be at least 1/16" in height.

If the total surface area is less than 5 square inches it can be reduced to not less than 1/32" high.

For an off-package ingredient listing for direct mail cosmetics (see Chapter 10) the ingredient listing must be 3/16" high.

See Chapter 4 for examples of type sizes and how to measure them.

Clear and easy to read

The ingredient list must be able to be read with ease by an average person under normal conditions of purchase.

You can't obscure the ingredient listing by overlapping or crowding it with any kind of design, background or image. It must have sufficient contrast with the background that it can be easily read.

The type face should be of sufficient resolution that it can be read even when small. In some cases, home ink-jet printers that have low resolution will cause blurring or distortion on very small text, thus making it in violation of the regulations.

Identification of Ingredients

The way an ingredient is named in the ingredient list must be understandable to the consumer. In order to keep the names somewhat standardized, the FDA has a system for how to determine the name.

First, some ingredients have had specific names established by the FDA Commissioner and included in the regulations. These are mostly very chemical names, so they are not listed in this book. If you are using any of these ingredients, your supplier should be able to give you the right name to use and your chemist and/or attorney should be familiar with the labeling requirements.

A color additives must be listed by the approved name. See Appendix A for more information.

For all other ingredients, the name to use should be taken from[1]:

---

[1] For more information about the different entities listed here, see the Glossary.

a) The *Cosmetic Ingredient Dictionary* published by the Cosmetic, Toiletry and Fragrance Association[1] (known as the INCI[2] name)

b) *United States Pharmacopeia*

c) *National Food Formulary*

d) *Food Chemical Codex*

e) USAN and the USP Dictionary of Drug Names

If the ingredient is not listed in any of those sources, then it should be written as:

f) The name generally recognized by consumers, or

g) The chemical or technical name or description.

Most cosmetic ingredients are listed in the *Cosmetic Ingredient Dictionary*, which is the standard in the industry.

Cosmetic Ingredient Dictionary Editions

The current FDA regulations refer to the 2nd edition of the International Cosmetic Ingredient Dictionary (published in 1977). Therefore listings correct in the 2nd and 3rd editions are legally correct on any product label.

Subsequent editions, have not yet been recognized nor adopted by the FDA, but the FDA has stated they will accept labeling of products in accordance with later editions. So you have a choice as to which bersion you choose to use.

Format of Botanical Names

From the 2nd to the 5th editions of International Cosmetic Ingredient Dictionary, the correct form for a botanical ingredient was the common English name.

---

[1] In late 2007 the Cosmetic, Toiletry and Fragrance Association changed their name to the Personal Care Council.

[2] INCI: International Nomenclature of Cosmetic Ingredients. It is the standardized name for referring to a particular cosmetic ingredient.

> ***Examples:*** Peppermint Oil
> Sweet Almond Oil
> Shea Butter

With the publication of the 6th edition, an attempt was undertaken to standardize botanical names so they would be understandable throughout different cultures and languages. The 6th edition required the Latin name for the botanical to be placed in parenthesis after the common name.

> ***Examples:*** Peppermint (Mentha Peperita) Oil
> Apricot Kernel (Prunus armeniaca) oil
> Shea (Butyrospermum parkii) butter

By the time the 8th edition was published, American consumers had gotten used to looking at the Latin names in addition to the common names. So starting in the 8th edition, the format was changed to show the Latin name of the botanical is first, followed by the common name in parenthesis.

The current edition follows the format of the 8th edition and uses the botanical name, followed by the common name either in parenthesis or with a slash (/) followed by the part of the plant used (if known) and the form the ingredient was in.

> ***Examples:*** Mentha Peperita (Peppermint) leaf oil
> Prunus armeniaca (Apricot) kernel oil
> Prunus armeniaca/Apricot seed powder
> Rosa damascena/Rose petals
> Olea europaea (Olive) oil
> Citrus aurantifolia/Lime peel powder
> Lavandula angustifolia/Lavender distillate water

Which is the Correct Format?

It is correct to use the simple form of the botanical INCI name as listed in the 2nd to 5th editions. It is also correct to use the listing with the latin name, in the format from either the 6th edition or the 8th edition and the different formats can be mixed-and-matched.

The most important fact is that the ingredient is currently written in a format that is in at least one of the INCI editions.

Appendix B contains a list of the currently accepted names for many common ingredients used by handcrafters and small businesses.

Fragrance and Flavor

Fragrance and flavor compounds may be written as "fragrance" or "flavor" respectively. If a fragrance ALSO serves as a flavor, then it must be written "flavor and fragrance".

You can choose to list the components (ingredients) of a flavor or fragrance individually by their appropriate names and place them in the ingredient list where they fit by amount in the cosmetic, but that is not required.

Any ingredient listed as a flavor or fragrance must be one that the consumer would commonly understand to be a flavor or fragrance. In other words, you can't obscure an ingredient by calling it a flavor or fragrance when it really isn't one.

Example - Fragrance (Body Powder)

Both ingredient listings are correct; one shows the essential oils used to make the fragrance listed in order of predominance, the other just uses "fragrance".

> Ingredients: Tapioca Starch, Cornstarch, Kaolin, Lavendula Officinalis (Lavender) Oil and Mentha Pepperita (Peppermint) Oil.

> Ingredients: Tapioca Starch, Cornstarch, Kaolin and Fragrance.

Masking Fragrance

An ingredient or mixture of ingredients added to mask an undesirable odor (but not add any noticeable scent) may be listed by its individual name(s) or as "fragrance".

Typically a product with a masking agent is still considered to be "fragrance free".

Trade Secrets

A "trade secret" is defined as:

Any formula, pattern, device or compilation of information which is used in one's business and which gives him an opportunity to obtain an advantage over competitors who do not know or use it.

A trade secret ingredient or formula doesn't have to be listed on the ingredients listing; instead you can say "and other ingredients".

However, in order to exempt listing an ingredient you must first get approval from the FDA. There is a very specific procedure for requesting exemption of an ingredient identity from public disclosure. The details are listed on the FDA website and available through local FDA offices.

If you omit an ingredient as a trade secret without having prior approval from the FDA then the product is misbranded and in violation of labeling regulations.

Incidental Ingredients

An incidental ingredient does not need to be declared on the label.

An "incidental ingredient" is:

1) A substance that has no technical or functional effect in the cosmetic but is present by reason of having been incorporated into the cosmetic as an ingredient of another cosmetic ingredient; or

2) A processing aid which is added to the cosmetic during processing but which is:

a) removed from the cosmetic according to Good Manufacturing practices before the cosmetic is packaged;

b) converted to a substance which is the same as a constituent of the declared ingredients and does not significantly increase the concentration of that constituent; or

c) added for its technical and functional effect in the processing but is present in the finished cosmetic at insignificant levels and does not have any technical or functional effect in that cosmetic.

Examples of Incidental Ingredients

» A defoaming agent that was added to an oil used in the cosmetic

» A preservative of a raw material added at so small a percentage that it is no longer effective

» A substance added as a filter aid and then removed

» Sodium hydroxide when added to a cosmetic that already contains stearic acid and sodium stearate (the sodium hydroxide and stearic acid combine into sodium stearate which is already on the label)

Note that the "incidental ingredient" must be truly incidental; this special circumstance can't be used to omit an ingredient that should otherwise be disclosed to the consumer.

Blended Ingredients

Where one ingredient is a combination of several components, then each component is considered a unique ingredient and should be added in the correct order based on the amount in the final product.

If you purchase a base or blended ingredient and include that in your product, you must get enough information from your supplier or the manufacturer to place the ingredients on your ingredient list correctly (in descending order of predominance in the finished product).

Example - Combined Ingredients (Lotion)

Consider a lotion that includes a preservative blend at 1% and fragrance at .5%. An ingredient declaration in descending order cannot list the preservative blend in the 1% place on the list (before the fragrance) because the individual components or ingredients in the preservative blend are not more than .5% of the whole.

Incorrect:

> Ingredients: Water, almond oil, castor oil, emulsifying wax NF, propylene glycol (and) diazolidinyl urea (and) methylparaben (and) propylparaben, and fragrance.

Correct:

> Ingredients: Water, almond oil, castor oil, emulsifying wax NF, propylene glycol, fragrance, diazolidinyl urea, methylparaben, and propylparaben.

The individual ingredients in the preservative blend must be listed separately. Using the descending order of predominance, the fragrance is listed after propylene glycol and before diazolidinyl urea. (Ingredients that are present at less than 1% also have an alternative listing sequence—see Chapter 8.)

Cosmetics That Are Also Drugs

If a cosmetic is also a drug, the label must follow drug labeling guidelines. Drug labeling is not covered in this book.

Chapter 8

Order of Ingredients in the Declaration

The general rule is that all ingredients are listed in descending order of predominance. This is considered the "conventional" listing and is always correct.

In other words, the ingredient of which there is the most in the cosmetic (the highest percentage) is listed first, the next most used ingredient goes second, etc.

If you list the ingredients that way, you won't go wrong.

Alternatives and Exceptions

There are a few alternative listing options and some exceptions to the descending order of predominance requirement that make creating the ingredient declaration a bit easier. The execeptions and options concern:

a) ingredients at less than 1%

b) color additives

c) alternative ingredients

d) colors for color matching

e) packages of several items

As a result of these various exceptions, there are sometimes several different ways to list the ingredients, all of which are correct.

Less Than 1%

Ingredients present at a concentration not exceeding 1% may be listed in any order after the listing of ingredients present at more than 1%.

Using the example from the previous chapter (a lotion with a preservative blend at 1% and fragrance at .5%), you see that all the constituents of the preservative blend and the fragrance are at less than 1% concentration. Therefore they could be listed in any order after the other ingredients.

Correct Example:

> Ingredients: Water, almond oil, castor oil, emulsifying wax NF, fragrance, propylene glycol, diazolidinyl urea, methylparaben and propylparaben.

Correct Example:

> Ingredients: Water, almond oil, castor oil, emulsifying wax NF, propylene glycol, diazolidinyl urea, methylparaben, propylparaben and fragrance.

Color Additives

Color additives, no matter the amount, may be listed in any order after all the non-color ingredients.

> **Only ingredients which are approved as color additives may be treated as such on the ingredient listing.**

An ingredient that is added to the product that happens to change the final color, but is not an approved color additive, must be listed in the appropriate place in descending order of predominance. (See Chaper 13 and Appendix A for additional information on color additives.)

Correct Example:

Soap with 2% mica (an approved colorant) added to make the soap brown (even though that may be a higher percentage than the fragrance):

> Ingredients: water, palm oil, coconut oil, sodium hydroxide, olive oil, fragrance and mica.

Correct Example:

Soap with 2% cocoa powder added which happens to turn the soap brown (but is not an approved color additive).

> Ingredients: water, palm oil, coconut oil, sodium hydroxide, olive oil, cocoa powder and fragrance.

Alternative Ingredients

If you know there is a current or anticipated shortage of an ingredient, you can specify an alternative on the ingredient listing, either within the ingredient list or at the end of the list.

Alternative Ingredient Within the Ingredient List

Place the alternative ingredient after the normally used ingredient at the appropriate place in the ingredient list, after the word "or".

Correct Example:

> Ingredients: water, palm oil, (coconut oil or palm kernel oil), sodium hydroxide, olive oil, fragrance, mica.

Alternative Ingredient After the Ingredients List

The alternative ingredient can be placed at the end of the ingredients list, after the words "May also contain".

Correct Example:

> Ingredients: water, palm oil, coconut oil, sodium
> hydroxide, olive oil, fragrance, mica. May also contain
> palm kernel oil.

Limitations on Alternative Ingredients

You may not use an alternative ingredient declaration in the ingredient list if the original ingredient is mentioned on any other label panel or in advertising for the product.

For example, if your label or advertising says that your cream contains shea butter, you can't include an alternative ingredient statement that cocoa butter might replace the shea butter.

Color Matching

If you sometimes add a color additive to a cosmetic during manufacture for the purpose of color matching, it may be listed on the ingredients list even if it isn't in every batch.

In that case, you would put the color after all the other colors after the phrase "May contain".

Correct Example:

A lip balm that uses beeswax or carnauba and may need additional color additive to keep the product color standard depending on the type of wax used.

> Ingredients: (Beeswax or Carnauba Wax), lanolin,
> castor oil, shea butter, Titanium Dioxide, Ultrama-
> rines, Red 21. May contain Red 22

Packages of Several Items

When a consumer cosmetic product contains a combination of items within it, the consumer still has to be able to see all the ingredients of all the products in the package.

Outer Container

All the ingredients must be declared on the outside package. That means that all the ingredients for all the included items must be on the outer wrapper so the consumer can see them when deciding to purchase the product or not.

Inner (Immediate) Container

If the individual containers within the package are normally separated from the outside container for individual retail sale, then the ingredients must also be declared on the inside (immediate) containers of each different cosmetic product.

If the package is never separated and is only sold as a single unit, then the ingredients do not need to be put on the inside (immediate) containers of the products.

Combined Ingredient Lists

In order to reduce repetitive ingredient statements on a label, when there are two or more individual products within a single package, the ingredient lists may be combined.

Exactly how they go together depends on whether the package contains similar or dissimilar items, the size of the label surface and whether or not it is a branded shade line[1].

The possibilities are:

- Dissimilar products
- Similar products intended for the same use
  - Label is less than 12 square inches
  - Label is more than 12 square inches
- Branded Shade Line
  - Single Unit
  - Assortment

---

[1] A branded shade line is a series of products of similar composition, intended for the same use, and sharing a common label with the same brand name and the only difference being color.

The Simplest Way

Remember, the conventional ingredient declaration, where each ingredient is listed in descending order of predominance, is always correct. On packages that contain multiple items the only difference is that you need to identify which item you are listing ingredients for.

Assortment of Dissimilar Items

There are two types of assortments of dissimilar items, depending on their final use.

Multi-Component Package

A multi-component package is:

> *A package of different items that combine together to make a complete kit, which is delivered in the form of an application.*

Examples of Multi-Component Packages:

- » A hair color kit of dye solution and mixing base
- » Face mask kit made up of clays, glycerine solution and essential oil blend.

Multi-Unit Package (Dissimilar Items)

A multi-unit package of dissimilar items is:

> *A package of items that go together, but are not alike. This is similar to a "variety pack" for the quantity of contents statement.*

Examples of Multi-Unit Packages

- » A shaving cream and an after shave lotion
- » Gift set of bubble bath and after-bath lotion
- » Gift basket of sugar scrub, soap and body powder

An assortment of dissimilar items may bear either the conventional or alternative ingredient listing.

Conventional Ingredient Listing

Each ingredient is listed in descending order of predominance under a heading indicating which product it is in. It would also be correct to use the alternative conventional listing, with items at a quantity of less than 1% listed in any order and the color additives, regardless of amount, listed after that.

Alternative Ingredient Listing

In the alternative ingredient listing, each ingredient except color additives is listed for each product under an appropriate product heading. Following that, the color additives that are in all the products are listed with a statement that the color additives apply to all products.

The alternative ingredient listing can save space on the label if the same color additives are used in all the products.

Example - Assortment of Dissimilar Items

Gift set containing sugar scrub, soap and body powder which are colored using some of the same color additives.

The individual ingredient lists are:

Scrub	Soap	Powder
Almond Oil	Palm Oil	Tapioca Starch
Olive Oil	Coconut Oil	Corn Starch
Shea Butter	Sodium Hydroxide	Rice Starch
Fragrance	Olive Oil	Fragrance
Red 33	Shea Butter	Mica
Red 5	Fragrance	Red 33
Mica	Red 33	
	Mica	

Correct Example - Conventional Listing:

All ingredients listed under the product in which they are included.

Sugar Scrub Ingredients: Almond oil, olive oil, shea butter, fragrance, Red 33, Red 5, Mica.
Soap Ingredients: Palm oil, coconut oil, sodium hydroxide, olive oil, shea butter, fragrance, mica, Red 33
Body Powder: Tapioca Starch, corn starch, rice starch, fragrance, mica, Red 33

Correct Example - Alternative Listing:

All ingredients listed under the product in which they are included, with the colors for all products listed after with a statement that the color additives apply to all products.

Sugar Scrub Ingredients: Almond oil, olive oil, shea butter, fragrance, Red 5.
Soap Ingredients: Palm oil, coconut oil, sodium hydroxide, olive oil, shea butter, fragrance.
Body Powder: Tapioca Starch, corn starch, rice starch, fragrance.
Colors (all products) Red 33, mica.

Assortment of Similar Items

Similar products are ones which are the same kind of product but differ only in a minor way, such as color and/or fragrance, and are intended for the same use.

Example of Assortment of Similar Products

   » Two body powders of different fragrances

   » Set of eye shadows in different colors

   » Three different bar soaps

An assortment of similar products can be labeled with a conventional ingredient listing, but there are also two correct alternative listings, depending on the available label space.

Conventional Listing

Each ingredient is listed in descending order of predominance under a heading indicating which product it is in.

It would also be correct to use the alternative conventional listing, with items at a quantity of less than 1% listed in any order and the color additives listed after that.

Alternative Listing - Label More Than 12 Square Inches

If the available label space is more than 12 square inches, the alternative ingredient listing lists the ingredients in the following order:

1) **Common Ingredients:** Ingredients other than color that are common to all products, listed in descending order of predominance;

2) **Not Common Ingredients:** Ingredients other than color that are not common to all products, identified by the products they are in;

3) **Color Additives:** Color additives of all products without identification of which product they are in.

Remember that the text size must be greater than 1/16" when the available label space is greater than 12 square inches.

Alternative Listing - Label Less Than 12 Square Inches

If the available label space is less than 12 square inches, then all the ingredients of all products (other than color additives) may be combined into a single cumulative list and shown in descending order of predominance and then a combined list of all colors used.

Example - Assortment of Similar Items

A set of three different cosmetic bar soaps, each with the same base oils, but different additives.

Lavender Soap	Tea Tree Soap	Lemongrass Soap
Water	Water	Water
Palm Oil	Palm Oil	Palm Oil
Coconut Oil	Coconut Oil	Coconut Oil
Sodium Hydroxide	Sodium Hydroxide	Sodium Hydroxide
Olive Oil	Olive Oil	Olive Oil
Shea Butter	Castor Oil	Sunflower Oil
Lavender Oil	Tea Tree Oil	Lemongrass Oil
Ultramarines	Mica	Mica
Mica	Iron Oxide	Titanium Dioxide

Correct Example - Conventional Listing

Each product listed separately with its ingredients in descending order of predominance.

> **Lavender Soap:** Water, palm oil, coconut oil, sodium hydroxide, olive oil, shea butter, lavender oil, ultramarine violet, mica.
> **Tea Tree Soap:** Water, palm oil, coconut oil, sodium hydroxide, olive oil, castor oil, tea tree oil, mica, iron oxide.
> **Lemongrass Soap:** Water, palm oil, coconut oil, sodium hydroxide, olive oil, sunflower oil, lemongrass oil, mica, titanium dioxide.

Correct Example - Larger Label:

First the ingredients common to all products in descending order of predominance, then the not-common ingredients identified by the product they are in, then the color additives (without identifying which product).

> Ingredients: Water, palm oil, coconut oil, sodium hydroxide, olive oil, shea butter and lavender oil in lavender soap, castor oil and tea tree oil in tea tree soap, sunflower oil and lemongrass oil in lemongrass soap, ultramarine violet, mica, iron oxide, titanium dioxide.

Correct Example - Smaller Label:

If the available label space is less than 12 square inches, then all ingredients in all products listed in descending order of predominance, followed by the color additives for all products.

> Ingredients: Water, palm oil, coconut oil, sodium hydroxide, olive oil, shea butter, castor oil, sunflower oil, lavender oil, tea tree, lemongrass oil, ultramarine violet, mica, iron oxide, titanium dioxide.

Branded Shade Lines & Assortments

The definition of a "branded shade line" is:

A series of products of similar composition, intended for the same use, and sharing a common label with the same brand name and the only difference being the color.

Only eye makeup (i.e.eyeshadow, eye liner, mascara, eye make-up remover,) non-eye make-up preparations (i.e. blusher, face powders, foundations, body paints, lipstick) and nail polish and enamel qualify as branded shade products.

What makes them a branded shade line or assortment is the fact that they all have the same brand, same ingredients and the same label; all that changes is the particular color or group of colors.

They can be individually packaged or in a package containing one or several assortments.

Examples of Branded Shade Lines & Assortments

- » One lipstick out of a line of lipsticks with the same brand name
- » A single compact containing several eye shadow colors
- » A set of several compacts each containing several eye shadow colors
- » One nail color out of a line of nail colors with the same brand name
- » A pack of three nail colors of the same line

Items in a branded shade line and branded shade line assortment may bear either a conventional ingredient declaration or an alternative ingredient listing.

Conventional Listing for Branded Shades

There are two possible conventional labels, depending on the type of product.

1) For an individual product, the label may show the ingredient listing for that product as per the normal requirements for a product label.

2) For an assortment, the label may show a combined list of all ingredients in a single list for that particular assortment (See Assortments of Similar Products, above).

Alternative Listing for Branded Shades

When using the alternative listing, each shade of a branded shade line or each package of a branded shade line assortment bears the same ingredient declaration.

In other words, if you were looking at a set of 5 different lipsticks in a branded line, all would have the exact same wording on the ingredient list.

The alternate ingredient declaration allows for listing all ingredients for all branded shades, as follows:

1) **Ingredients common to all products**, in cumulative descending order of predominance

2) **Ingredients not common**, identified by the product in which they are used

3) **Color additives common to all products**, in any order

4) **Color additives not common**, preceded by "may contain"

CORRECT EXAMPLE - Branded Shade Line

Lipstick line, used as an example.

Ingredients: Castor Oil, Isopropyl Myristate, Beeswax, Candelilla Wax, Oleyl Alcohol, Ozokerite, Sorbitan Trioleate (in Pearl Peach and Pearl Cherry Shades), Titanium Dioxide, Red 21, Orange 5.
May Contain: Iron oxides, Red 6 Barium Lake, Red 7 Calcium Lake, Red 27 Aluminum Lake, Orange 5 Aluminum Lake, Yellow 10 Aluminum Lake

---

Chapter 9
Ingredient Declarations for Soap

Soap as a product has a multi-personality complex. It can be a consumer product, a cosmetic or even a drug—all depending on how it is presented to to public. And remember, that's the consumer's idea of the intended use. Chapter 2 goes into detail on how to determine what the soap is.

Keeping It Simple

If you stick to the exact requirements for the soap label, based on the type of product it is, it's pretty easy.

Remember, if there are no cosmetic claims, the soap is a non-cosmetic consumer product (i.e. just a "soap") and no ingredient listing is required. If there are cosmetic claims, then it is a cosmetic and all cosmetic labeling rules, including a declaration of ingredients, must be followed. In all cases, the name and identity of the product, the business name/address and quantity of contents are required.

Soap Ingredients

Sometimes ingredients react with one another upon mixing in a formulation, and create something new. Such is the case with soap; when oils and lye (sodium hydroxide) are combined, they chemically change and become soap.

The FDA has ruled that an ingredient formed that way may be declared either by its "starting materials" or by the "reaction products."

In either event, the ingredient listing must use correct INCI names from the *Cosmetic Ingredient Dictionary* published by the Cosmetic, Toiletry and Fragrance Association (2nd to current edition) and it must be an accurate representation of the actual ingredients.

Saponified Oils

Soap is the result of the reaction between oil and lye, a process called "saponification". In casual conversation one can say that soap is "saponified oils", or to be even more detailed, a particular soap might be the "saponified oils of palm and olive" or "saponified palm and olive oils."

These statements are correct, but it is not correct terminology for an ingredient list.

"Saponified ____ oil" or **"Saponified oil of ____"** is not listed as an ingredient in any version of the *Cosmetic Ingredient Dictionary*.

The *Cosmetic Ingredient Dictionary* lists specific terms to describe the soap-result of saponification of a particular oil and sodium or potassium hydroxide.

> ***Examples:***   sodium palm kernelate
> sodium cocoate
> potassium olivate

Handcrafted Soap from Scratch

While sodium cocoate, sodium palmate and sodium olivate (and their counterpart-names for other saponified oils) form the basis of handcrafted soaps made from scratch (usually by cold or hot process), there's something more in them as well. Without going into the chemistry of soapmaking, suffice it to say that one of the benefits of handcrafted soaps is that there is a portion of the oil in them that **isn't** turned into soap.

In fact, many soapmakers intentionally add specialty oils at the end of the saponification process ("super-fatting") or decrease the amount of lye in order to leave unsaponified oils in the soap ("lye discount").

The good news is that those unsaponified oils are part of what makes handcrafted soaps so enjoyable. The bad news is that those unsaponified oils exist in the finished bar as constituents which are separate and distinct from the the soap itself (made up of the oils which have saponified).

Listing What Goes INTO the Soap Pot

The simplest, and generally most correct, way is to list the ingredients that you actually put into the soap pot. These would be what the FDA refers to as the "starting ingredients".

Correct Example (2nd edition INCI names):

Listing the simple, common name for botanical products (oils) as they went into the soap pot.

> Ingredients: Water, palm oil, coconut oil, sodium hydroxide, olive oil, fragrance, mica.

Correct Example (6th edition INCI names):

Listing the English name with the Latin name in parenthesis.

> Ingredients: Water, Palm (Elaeis guineensis) oil, Coconut (Cocos nucifera) oil, sodium hydroxide, Olive (Olea europaea) oil, fragrance, mica.

Correct Example (8th edition INCI names):

Listing the Latin name with the common English name in parenthesis.

> Ingredients: Water, Elaeis guineensis (palm) oil, Cocos nucifera (coconut) oil, sodium hydroxide, Olea europaea (olive) oil, fragrance, mica.

Listing What Comes OUT of the Soap Pot[1]

If you know what actually comes out of your soap pot, you could list that in the ingredients declaration. You would need to know the amount of each of the following constituents in the finished soap:

» each reacted ingredient (the saponified oil),

» glycerine resulting from the saponification of the oils (triglycerides)

» unsaponified oils/triglycerides

» remaining, unevaporated water

» fragrance, herbs, clays, colors or other additives

AND be able to correctly list them in descending order of predominance.

Conditionally Correct Example:

If you could test for the amount of glycerine and unsaponified palm, coconut, and olive oils, then this would be the correct format.

Ingredients: Sodium palmate, sodium cocoate, sodium olivate, water, fragrance, glycerine, palm oil, coconut oil, olive oil, fragrance, mica.

---

[1] Over the years handcrafted soap makers have maintained that they can control the unsaponified oils in a finished bar of soap. It is a commonly held opinion that there is a difference in the resultant soap when the total amount of lye is discounted to leave some oils unsaponfied and when additional oils are added at trace, after the saponification process has started. The theory is that oils added at trace will remain in the finished product as unsaponified oils.

Kevin Dunn, PhD, Elliott Professor of Chemistry at Hampden-Sydney College, and his students researched to determine the difference, if any, between soaps made with the lye-discount method and the super-fat method. The result of their research was presented at the 2007 Annual Conference of the Handcrafted Soap Makers Guild and published in 4th Quarter 2007 issue of *The Handcrafted Soapmaker*, journal of the Handcrafted Soap Makers Guild, Inc.

They found that the unsaponified oils in lye-discounted and super-fatted soaps were virtually identical. In other words, it made no difference in the resultant soap if the specialty oils were added at trace or at the beginning of the mix. That being the case, adding the oils at trace is not a valid method for determining what unsaponified oils remain in the finished bar.

Liquid Soap

Handcrafted (and other) liquid soap that is made with potassium hydroxide, water and oil, is often made using a process that ensures that there are no unsaponified oils remaining in the soap (to increase the clarity of the soap).

If the soap has been made in that manner, then it would not incorrect to list the INCI name for the saponified oil, provided the amount of resultant glycerine has also been determined.

Correct Example:

Ingredients: Water, potassium cocoate, potassium olivate, fragrance, glycerine.

Also Correct Example:

Ingredients: Water, coconut oil, olive oil, potassium hydroxide, fragrance.

Commercial Soap Base

Handling the ingredient listing for a soap product made with a commerically purchased soap base depends on two factors:

1) If the base is NOT a soap, by the FDA definition, or
2) If cosmetic claims been made for the product.

If the either of the above statements are TRUE, then the ingredients must be listed on the product.

Usually a person making a product starting with a commercial soap base produces a unique product by adding specialty ingredients, fragrance and/or color to the base. While he/she knows the percentage of fragrance or color, he/she may not know the percentage of all the ingredients used by the manufacturer to create the soap base.

The manufacturer of the product should provide an accurate ingredient declaration. In fact, if the soap base is not a soap by the FDA definition, it must be labeled as a cosmetic (including an ingredient list) when it is shipped.

The manufacturer should also provide sufficient information about the formulation to enable the person producing the final product to accurately place their additives in the correct order within the ingredient listing.

Soap as a Non-Cosmetic Consumer Commodity

As discussed earlier, soap is a consumer commodity (and therefore not regulated by the FDA) when:

1) It is a soap, by the FDA definition, AND

2) No cosmetic claims been made for the product (on the product or in the accompanying materials)

A non-cosmetic consumer commodity does not require an ingredient listing. Sometimes, however, a soap maker wants to say what's in the soap.

> **Putting an ingredient listing on a soap does not make it a cosmetic[1].**

Acceptable Options to the Ingredient List

It wouldn't hurt anything to put the full ingredient listing, following all the FDA rules and regulations on the soap label. However, it is not required.

In fact, technically, since the FDA does not regulate soap, and the FTC does not require or regulate ingredient lists, there are no requirements on how the ingredients of a non-cosmetic soap may be presented.

---

[1] Because there have been many statements made contrary to this over the years, the author specifically checked it with the FDA Cosmetic Compliance Division to clarify whether putting the ingredient list on a soap product causes it to become considered a cosmetic. It does not.

If a product is a soap by the FDA definition, the ONLY way it becomes a cosmetic is if cosmetic claims are made for it. It doesn't matter if the ingredients are on the label; by itself, that does not constitute a cosmetic claim.

You could choose to present the information about what's in the soap in a different format or use different ingredient names than would be required for a cosmetic.

Here are some optional ways that might be used to tell the consumer what is in the product:

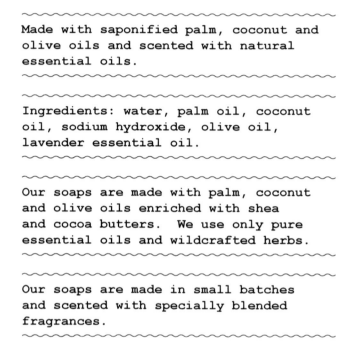

Made with saponified palm, coconut and olive oils and scented with natural essential oils.

Ingredients: water, palm oil, coconut oil, sodium hydroxide, olive oil, lavender essential oil.

Our soaps are made with palm, coconut and olive oils enriched with shea and cocoa butters. We use only pure essential oils and wildcrafted herbs.

Our soaps are made in small batches and scented with specially blended fragrances.

Keep it Truthful

Even though you are not required to list all the ingredients in the typical cosmetic-label format, it doesn't mean that you are allowed to present the information in a way that is intended to deceive the consumer.

Most consumers don't realize that there are different rules for soap and cosmetics. They have come to expect that when the product says "Ingredients" the list will be complete and generally in descending order of predominance. If you intentionally create an ingredient list that looks like it is all-inclusive and then leave something important off, you could be accused of deceptive labeling practices – not by the FDA (who doesn't have juristiction) but by the Fair Trade Commission (who does have juristiction over soap).

Consumer Safety

There is also a safety issue. Consumers, particularly those with allergies or sensitivities, look to the packaging to determine if they can use the product. If the wording on the package implies that all the ingredients are listed when they aren't really all included, then the consumer might think the product was safe for her when it was not.

If you don't use a complete ingredient description in the cosmetic product format, make sure that what you do say accurately conveys to the consumer whether it is a complete list of ingredients or not.

Accidental Cosmetic Claims

Remember that a cosmetic claim can be made anywhere on the package or in accompanying information (including promotional materials or statements on your website).

Watch out for accidental cosmetic claims similar to these:

> "Made with saponified palm, coconut and olive oils, with moisturizing shea butter added"

> "Handcrafted soaps don't remove the glycerin from the soap, so you get the moisturizing benefits of the naturally-occurring glycerin in every bar."

> "Our soaps are made with a unique blend of emollient vegetable oils"

> "Gently cleans and softens rough skin"

> "Ingredients: water, palm oil, coconut oil, sodium hydroxide, olive oil, glycerine (humectant), cocoa butter and fragrance."

> "Based on the long tradition of Shea Butter providing moisturizing and skin care benefits, we include Shea Butter in all our products."

Chapter 10

Ingredient Declaration: Special Circumstances

There are some other special circumstances that may affect the way the ingredient list is handled. In some cases you don't even have to put the ingredient list on the package!

Revised Formulation

If you change your formula, you can still use packages or labels with the old ingredient list if you attach a revised ingredient declaration.

The revised list must be on either:

a) a firmly affixed tag, tape, sticker, card or similar overlabeling that says "New Ingredient List" conspicuously with letters at least 1/16" high; OR

b) labeling inside an unsealed package AND a sticker or some other overlabel on the outside package that says "New Ingredient List" conspicuously with letters at least 1/16" high.

Direct Mail Off-Package Ingredient List

Direct mail cosmetics may have off-package ingredient labeling instead of putting the ingredients list directly on the package.

The definition of "direct mail cosmetics" is:

Cosmetics distributed to consumers by direct mail without involvement of an intermediary sales agent.

Cosmetics sold to consumers by "door-to-door" salespersons or at home parties are not considered direct mail cosmetics even though they may be delivered to consumers directly by mail.

Cosmetics sold on a website and delivered directly to the consumer are considered direct mail cosmetics.

Ingredient List

Instead of declaring the ingredients on the information panel, for direct mail cosmetics the ingredients declaration may be in:

a) Materials that come with the cosmetic, such as a brochure, insert or written directions for safe use; and/or

b) Labeling furnished to the consumer for personal use and from which cosmetics are ordered, i.e. a direct mail sales catalog, brochure or web page.

In both cases the text of the ingredients declaration must be at least 3/16" high.

Special Requirements

If the ingredients of direct mail cosmetics are on off-package labeling, the following requirements must also be met:

1) The package mailed to consumers must be accompanied by a notice in 3/16" lettering that tells the consumer:

- The location of the ingredient declaration(s),
- Name & address of the mail order distributor,
- That a copy of the ingredient declaration(s) will be mailed to any person requesting it.

2) The notice must be on or attached to the top of the package or it must be inside the package on top of the contents so it is immediately visible when the package is opened by the consumer.

3) The mail order distributor must promptly mail a copy of an ingredient declaration to any person requesting it.

4) The ingredient declarations must be conspicuous and presented in a way that the consumer can readily associate each ingredient declaration with each cosmetic.

Retail Off-Package Ingredient Labeling

In certain circumstances retail packages may be displayed with off-package ingredient labeling. In order to qualify, the product must:

a) not be enclosed in an outer container; and

b) have a total package surface of less than 12 sq. inches; and

c) be held for sale in tightly compartmented trays or racks.

Eye or Facial Makeup Cosmetics or Nail Enamel

To qualify for an off-package ingredient listing, eye or facial make-up cosmetics or nail enamels may be held for sale in tightly compartmented trays or racks located below the sales counter. However, even if the product is held below the sales counter, the ingredient labeling must be in a holder of some kind and be attached to a display chart which bears samples of the product shades and is displayed to purchasers. In other words, you can't put the samples on the counter and the ingredient listing with the products under the counter.

Other Cosmetic Products

To qualify for an off-package ingredient listing, products other than eye or facial make-up cosmetics or nail enamels must be displayed for sale in tightly compartmented trays or racks of a display unit with the ingredient listing attached to the display unit and accessible to the consumer.

Unwrapped ("Naked") Soaps

When unwrapped ("naked") soaps are displayed for retail sale in a bin or tray, they qualify for off-package ingredient labeling.

Additional Requirements for an Off-Package Ingredient Listing

For retail off-package ingredient listing, the sheets, leaflets or other labeling containing the ingredient list must be in letters at least 1/16" in height and must be attached to the front of the display rack (except as noted below).

Several other conditions apply for off-package ingredient labeling:

1) The display unit or chart must bear the statement "Federal law requires ingredient lists to be displayed here" in letters not less than 3/16 of an inch in height. The statement must be visible when the last ingredient list has been taken. Alternatively, the statement may be shown at all times next to the labeling holder.

2) The holder of the off-package cosmetic ingredient labeling must be attached to the display unit or chart so that the labeling is in front of the display unit or chart and can be read in full by a purchaser facing the display under customary conditions of retail sale.

   As an alternative to having the off-package ingredient labeling in front of the display unit, the labeling may be placed on the side of the display unit or chart (but not at the top, back or bottom). If it's located on the side, there must be a conspicuous notice in 3/16" lettering on the front of the display unit saying where the off-package labeling is located and also stating "Federal law requires ingredient lists to be displayed here."

3) The sheets or leaflets attached to the display unit or chart must declare the ingredients of all products sold within the display.

4) The sheets or leaflets must be identical.

5) If you are selling wholesale, you must provide enough copies of the sheets or leaflets with each shipment so that each purchaser can get a copy of the ingredient declaration.

6) Shipments of refill items also must be accompanied by sufficient copies of ingredient declarations.

   The container holding the refill items and the respective copies of ingredient declarations must not contain other cosmetic products.

7) You must promptly mail a copy of the ingredient declaration to any person requesting it.

8) If the product formulation changes, the new sheets or leaflets must be dated if they are not shipped together with the display unit or chart.

   If a sheet or leaflet is to be used in conjunction with both the old and the new formulations, it must bear both ingredient declarations, and the declarations must be identified in a way that the purchaser can determine which ingredient list goes with which product.

   As an alternative, the sheet or leaflet bearing the two ingredient declarations may advise the purchaser that the formulation has been changed and that either declaration may be applicable.

Chapter 11
Required Warning Statements

When a cosmetic might be hazardous to the consumer if it is misused, then it must have appropriate label warnings and adequate directions for safe use. Any required warning statement must be prominent and conspicuous, so the consumer will see it. Type size must be at least 1/16".

Some situations and cosmetics are required by regulation to have specific warnings or cautions.

Unsubstantiated Safety Warning

The FD&C Act does not require that cosmetic manufacturers or marketers test their products for safety. However, as a manufacturer, it is common sense that you should know if your product is safe under normal use. You should also know how it might be misused and have some idea if it's safe in those circumstances. In addition, you should have some kind of substantiation of whether the product is safe.

If all the ingredients have been previously tested and proven to be "generally regarded as safe" (GRAS), then one could consider that the final product is also GRAS. The supplier of a particular ingredient should be able to tell you if the ingredient is GRAS and supply an MSDS sheet for the ingredient.

If untested ingredients are used, new and untested ingredient interations created, or the safety of the cosmetic overall cannot be adequately substantiated, then the product safety is considered unsubstantiated and the product must include a warning label.

The Unsubstantiated Warning Label must be displayed on the Primary Display Panel and contain the following text:

> Warning: The safety of this product has not been determined.

Foaming Detergent Bath Product (Bubble Bath)

Bubble bath or a "foaming detergent bath product" is defined as:

Any product intended to be added to a bath for the purpose of producing foam that contains a surface-active agent serving as a detergent or foaming ingredient.

Any bubble bath product that is not **clearly labeled for use by adults only** must have the following caution statement included on the label.

> Caution: Use only as directed. Excessive use or prolonged exposure may cause irritation to skin and urinary tract. Discontinue use if rash, redness or itching occurs. Consult your physician if irritation persists. Keep out of reach of children.

A bubble bath product must also have adequate directions for safe use of the product on the product packaging.

For Adults Only

To identify the bubble bath product as being intended for use by adults only, "**Keep out of reach of children**" or "**For adult use only**" m may be used.

Bubble Bath for Children

If the bubble bath product is intended for use by children, the phrase "Keep out of reach of children" may be expanded to further read "except under adult supervision" so the label would then read:

> Caution: Use only as directed. Excessive use or prolonged exposure may cause irritation to skin and urinary tract. Discontinue use if rash, redness or itching occurs. Consult your physician if irritation persists. Keep out of reach of children except under adult supervision.

Tanning Products Without Sunscreen

A "suntanning preparation" is a gel, cream, liquid or other topical product that is intended to provide a cosmetic effect on the skin (such as moisturizing or conditioning) while tanning OR that gives the appearance of a tan by changing the skin color through the use of color additives approved for that application.

Because consumers generally use such products at the beach or in a tanning salon, if they aren't paying attention they could think they are being protected by a sunscreen when they are not. In order to help keep consumers informed, the FDA requires the following warning label on any product sold or promoted as a "suntanning" type product that does not contain sunscreen:

> Warning: This product does not contain a sunscreen and does not protect against sunburn. Repeated exposure of unprotected skin while tanning may increase the risk of skin aging, skin cancer, and other harmful effects to the skin even if you do not burn.

Cosmetic Aerosols

A cosmetic product that is packaged in a self-pressurized container and intended to be expelled from the package under pressure must bear a warning label saying:

> Warning: Avoid spraying in eyes. Contents under pressure. Do not puncture or incinerate. Do not store at temperature above 120°F. Keep out of reach of children.

Glass Container

If the product is in a glass container, the word "puncture" may be replaced by the word "break". The label would then read:

> Warning: Avoid spraying in eyes. Contents under pressure. Do not break or incinerate. Do not store at temperature above 120°F. Keep out of reach of children.

Children's Product

If the product is intended for use by children, the phrase "except under adult supervision" may be added at the end of the last sentence of the warning:

> Warning: Avoid spraying in eyes. Contents under pressure. Do not puncture or incinerate. Do not store at temperature above 120°F. Keep out of reach of children except under adult supervision.

Product not expelled as a spray

If the product is not expelled as a spray (like an aerosol shave cream), the words "Avoid spraying in eyes" may be omitted. In that case the warning label should read:

> Warning: Contents under pressure. Do not puncture or incinerate. Do not store at temperature above 120°F. Keep out of reach of children.

Cosmetic Aerosols with Halocarbon or Hydrocarbon

If the propellant of a cosmetic packaged in a self-pressurized container consists partly or totally of a halocarbon or hydrocarbon, the label must bear an additional warning as stated below.

> Warning: Use only as directed. Intentional misuse by deliberately concentrating and inhaling the contents can be harmful or fatal.

However, this additional warning is not required for the following products:

1. Aerosol foam or cream products containing less than 10% propellant

2. Products which do not expel the propellant at the time of use. Examples: products with built-in piston barrier or propellant bag

3. Metered spray products of less than 2 oz. net contents

4. Aerosol products of less than 1/2 oz. net contents

Feminine Deodorant Sprays

A feminine deodorant spray is defined as:

Any spray deodorant product whose labeling represents or suggests that the product is for use in the female genital area or for use all over the body.

Any feminine deodorant spray must have the warning:.

> Caution: For external use only. Spray at least 8 inches from skin. Do not apply to broken, irritated, or itching skin. Persistent, unusual odor or discharge may indicate conditions for which a physician should be consulted. Discontinue use immediately if rash, irritation, or discomfort develops.

No halocarbon or hydrocarbon propellant

If the expelled product does not contain a liquefied halocarbon or hydrocarbon propellant, the sentence "Spray at least 8 inches from skin" may be omitted, making the label read:

> Caution: For external use only. Do not apply to broken, irritated, or itching skin. Persistent, unusual odor or discharge may indicate conditions for which a physician should be consulted. Discontinue use immediately if rash, irritation, or discomfort develops.

Using "hygiene" or "hygienic"

The word "hygiene" or "hygienic" or similar words may not be used on the product label of a feminine deodorant product. To use these words renders the product misbranded.

Chapter 12
Other Label Claims

Some claims are regulated by the FDA, FTC, EPA or other agency. In order to use the word or statement on your label you must meet very specific qualifications.

"Edible"

If you claim that a cosmetic product is "edible" then it is classed as a food and must be labeled in accordance with food labeling regulations.

"FDA Approved"

No cosmetic may be labeled or advertised with statements which suggest that the FDA has approved the product. To do so makes the product misbranded.

"Organic"

The National Organic Program, which falls under the United States Department of Agriculture (USDA) regulates the use of the term **"organic"** on any product, including personal care products.

A penalty of up to $10,000 can be levied on any person who knowingly sells or labels as organic a product that is not produced and handled in accordance with the National Organic Program's regulations.

Only an operation that has been officially certified as meeting organic standards may put the word "organic" on the principal display panel, label its products as organic or use the "USDA Organic" seal.

Organic Ingredient(s)

If you do not have a certified operation, you can still identify an organic ingredient on the ingredient list.

Example:

Ingredients: Tapioca Starch, Cornstarch, Kaolin, organic Lavendula Officinalis (Lavender) Oil and Mentha Pepperita (Peppermint) Oil.

Percentage of Organic Ingredients

In addition, you may state the percentage of organic ingredients on an informational panel on the package (but not on the principal display panel) using the statement:

Example:

x% organic ingredients

Note: Water, salt and lye (sodium hydroxide or potassium hydroxide) may not be counted as organic ingredients.

"Made in the USA"

If you want to make the claim that a product is "Made in the USA" you must comply with the Federal Trade Commission's *Made in the USA* policy. The FTC enforcement policy applies to all claims on products and labeling, advertising, promotional material, email and website statements.

In order to qualify as "Made in the USA", all the significant parts and processes that go into the product must be of US origin and the final processing and assembly must be in the US.

Product made from imported raw ingredients do not qualify for the "Made in the USA" claim.

If you intend to use the "Made in the USA" claim, then be sure to check with all your suppliers to find out the actual source of the ingredients you use. The determining factor is where the ingredient was manufactured - not where you purchased it.

Qualified "Made in the USA" Statements

In some cases you can make a qualified statement that indicates how much of the product was made in and from US products. The claim must be truthful and able to be substantiated.

"Introductory Offer"

The term "introductory offer" means:

Any printed matter consisting of the words "introductory offer" or words of similar import, placed upon a package containing any new commodity or upon any label affixed or adjacent to such new commodity, stating or representing by implication that such new commodity is offered for retail sale at a price lower than the anticipated ordinary and customary retail sale price.

In other words, if you say that the product is an "introductory offer" you are implying that the product will be available in the future and that the price will be higher at that time.

You may not print on a package that it's an "introductory offer" unless:

1) It's a new product, a product that has been significantly changed or is being offered into a trade area for the first time;

2) Each offer is clearly and conspicuously qualified (making it clear what the offer is);

3) A product labeled with "introductory offer" is not sold in a trade area for more than 6 months;

4) You intend to offer the same product in the same area for a period of time after the introductory offer is completed.

Introductory Offer - Record Keeping

If you print "Introductory Offer" on your packaging and follow the guidelines above, you must keep invoices or other records showing your compliance with the points above. The records must be available for inspection for 1 year after the introductory offer period ends.

Environmental Marketing Claims [1]

Environmental marketing (or "green") claims are monitored by the FTC. They look at it from the consumer's perspective and make sure that false or misleading claims are not made about a product or its packaging. They monitor the package, labeling, promotional materials, advertising and all aspects that relay information about the product to the consumer.

Substantiation

In order to make an environmental marketing claim you must be able to substantiate the claim and have a reasonable basis for making the claim.

Claims

Environmentally friendly claims must be fairly specific or clearly qualified where necessary. If a box containing a bottle of lotion is labeled "recycled" then it should be clear whether it is the box or the bottle or both that are made from recycled materials.

Broadly general claims like "eco-friendly," "environmentally preferable" or "environmentally safe" are harder to substantiate. They normally require some sort of qualifying statement.

---

1 In late 2007, the FTC initiated a review of their Evironmental Marketing Guides (called the "Green Guides"). As part of the Green Guides review, the FTC will be holding public meetings or workshops on a number of green marketing topics. The final revised document may be published as soon as early 2009.

"Non-Toxic"

According to the FTC, consumers understand claims that a product is "non-toxic," "essentially non-toxic" or "practically non-toxic" to mean that the toxicity claims apply not only to human health effects, but also to environmental effects. If a product poses a significant risk to humans or the environment then a non-toxic claim would be deceptive.

"Biodegradable"

A claim that a product is "biodegradable" or "degradable" means that the materials will break down and return to nature within a reasonably short time after customary disposal.

A product that goes down the drain would have to break down within the normal time of the wastewater treatment process. However, for products disposed of in a landfill it is difficult to determine what a "reasonably short time" would be because landfills are designed to reduce degradation of the items disposed of there.

Soap for consumer use is generally considered to be biodegradable so "biodegradable" could be used on a soap label if you wanted to.

Synthetic detergents are not necessarily biodegradable. If you are using a melt and pour soap that is detergent based, check with your supplier or manufacturer about the biodegradability of the product before placing the word on "biodegradable" your labeling.

"Compostable"

Composting turns degradable materials into usable compost—humus-like material that enriches the soil and returns nutrients to the earth. "Compostable" claims would be appropriate on products or packages that will break down and become part of usable compost in home compost piles in a safe and timely manner .

"Recyclable"

"Recyclable" claims on labels and advertisements generally mean that the package can be collected, separated or recovered from the solid waste stream and used again, or be reused in the manufacture

bly of another package or product through an established
; program.

It you make a "recyclable" claim on your packaging, you should
clearly state whether the claim refers to the product, the package, or
both.

For a product to be labeled "recyclable" without qualification,
the package and/or inner container must be able to be recycled in
most communities where it is sold. If it can't be recycled by most
everyone, then a qualifying statement like "*This bottle may not be
recyclable in your area*" must be included on the package.

A phrase like "*Recyclable where facilities exist*" is not a sufficient
qualifier.

"Please Recycle"

According to the FTC, when consumers see the phrase "*Please
Recycle*" on products they usually think it means that product or
package IS recyclable. Therefore, the same guidelines that apply to
putting "*recyclable*" on a package also apply to putting the words
"*Please Recycle*" on the package.

"Recycled Content"

"Recycled content" means that the product or package is made from
materials recovered or diverted from the solid waste stream —either
during the manufacturing process (pre-consumer) or after consumer
use (post-consumer).

Labels, packaging or advertising that state a product or package
contains recycled content must clearly indicate whether it is the
product or the package, if it is pre- or post-consumer content, and
what percentage of recycled content is used.

Recycle Symbol

If you use the recycle symbol, you should put a qualifier with it to
make it clear whether the package is recyclable or the product is
made with recycled materials.

In either case, the qualifier should follow the guidelines listed above.

110

"Refillable"

Claiming that the product is "refillable" can only be made if there is a way to collect and return the filled package or if the consumer can purchase a "refill" to go into the package.

"Reusable"

The FTC doesn't regulate the term "reusable". If the package can be reused in any way, the term may be used on the packaging or in product advertising.

Unregulated Terms

The FDA has tried to establish official definitions for some terms but so far the regulations have been overturned in court. According to the FDA website comment on unregulated terms:

"Companies can_use them on cosmetic labels to mean anything or nothing at all. Most of the terms have considerable market value in promoting cosmetic products to consumers, but dermatologists say they have very little medical meaning."

The un-regulated terms include:

Natural	Hypoallergenic
Alcohol Free	Cruelty Free
Fragrance Free	

In other words, there are no official, legal definitions for these un-regulated terms. What constitutes a natural, hypoallergenic, cruelty free product or ingredient is not specified by law. These are not scientific terms; they are marketing terms, defined and used to sell products.

The use of these unregulated terms, especially the term "natural," to describe both products and ingredients is so widespread that even consumers are beginning to realize there are no legal definitions for them and to question the truthfulness of the statements.

To meet the deman from consumers, several consumer groups in the US, Europe and Canada have started to sep in with various programs to certify products as "cruety free", "animal friendly", "eco-friendly", etc. The requirements for these certifications are established by the certifying organization, not any any government or regulatory agency and participation is completely optional (and sometimes with fees).

In early 2008 several large cosmetic companies in the US and Europe have created a group to create a standard for "natural" products. As of this writing, no definitive standards have been suggested or published.

If you choose to use any of the unregulated terms on your packaging, in your labeling or in your promotional materials, it's a good idea to clarify for the consumer exactly what you mean and to refer them to any private certifying organization with which you are participating.

Section 3

Other Important Things to Know

Chapter 13
Color Additives

An ingredient used specifically to change the color of a cosmetic product is called a "color additive". There is a strict system of regulation for color additives used in cosmetics.

Every color additive used in a cosmetic product must be on the FDA "approved list". Federal regulations specify which ingredients may be used as color additives and what products they may be used for. The regulations also cover the exact specifications for each color additive and any restrictions on its use.

To repeat that in different words, if you put an ingredient into a cosmetic product in order to change the color of the product, that ingredient is considered a "color additive". If it's not on the FDA approved list for that particular use, then you are breaking federal law and the FDA can come after you for producing and selling an adulterated product.

An ingredient used in a cosmetic for some specific reason other than to color the product that also happens to change the color of the product is not a color additive.

For example, your recipe for a Cappuccino Sugar Scrub calls for coffee grounds and brown sugar. When you add them, your scrub turns brown. The coffee grounds and brown sugar are not color additives.

However, if you made a Mint Julep Salt Scrub that used white salt and peppermint essential oil and then you added Chromium oxide green to make it a nice green color, that would be using a color additive.

The only thing that determines whether an ingredient is acceptable as a color additive is whether or not it is on the approved list. It does not matter if it is non-toxic, edible or anything else, only if it is on the approved color list. Crayons, "non-toxic" paint, food colors (unless you know the exact color additives used in them) and other similar products are not approved as color additives for cosmetics no matter how safe they may seem. Using them in any cosmetic product makes the product adulterated and the FDA can take action.

If you are purchasing your color additives from a reputable distributor, it is assumed that they are already approved to be used in cosmetics, have been certified (if required) and were produced within the specifications and guidelines required by law. Your supplier should be able to provide you with the required documentation on the color additive, including any restrictions on its use.

Ingredient Listings

Only an FDA approved color additive may be treated as a color additive in the ingredient listing. If the ingredient is not on the approved color additive list but happens to change the color of the product, it must be included with the regular ingredients in descending order of predominance in the ingredient declaration.

If the color additive is on the list of approved colors, it may be listed in the alternative ingredient declaration order, with the colors at the end of all of the other ingredients, regardless of the quantity in the product.

Types of Color Additives

Color additives are separated by regulation into two main categories: those that must be certified (sometimes called "certifiable") and those that do not have to be certified.

Colors Subject to Certification

Certifiable colors are primarily derived from petroleum and are sometimes known as "coal-tar dyes" or "synthetic-organic" colors.

The FDA's own labs must certify that the batch passed analysis for its composition and purity. If the batch is not FDA certified, it should not be used. The certification process is normally completed by the manufacturer of the color additive; you should never need to deal with certifying color additives.

A certified color generally has a three-part name: A prefix of FD&C (Food, Drug & Cosmetic), D&C (Drug & Cosmetic) or External D&C; a color; and a number. Example: FD&C Yellow No. 5. On ingredient declarations a certified color may be identified by just the color and number (i.e. "Yellow 5").

Don't confuse an FDA certification with the CI (Color Index) or E number sometimes used in European color identification. Only an FDA certification number meets the federal requirements in the US.

When purchasing certifiable colors, check the label on the package containing the color additive. The color's label must state the name of the color (i.e. "FD&C Yellow No. 5"). If the color is a mixture, the name of each ingredient must be listed. In addition, the FDA lot certification number and the color's uses and restrictions must be on the label of the package you receive from the supplier.

Note: Label your final consumer product in accordance with the labeling requirements set forth in earlier chapters of this book; you are not required to put the color certification information on the consumer product label.

Colors Exempt from Certification

Color additives that are exempt from certification are generally obtained from mineral, plant or animal sources. They are not subject to FDA testing or certification.

Even though they generally are derived from natural sources, they are still considered artificial colors. They are "artificial" because the product is changing color solely by the use of the color additive.

The color additive still might come from a completely "natural" source, but is still "artificially" changing the color of the product.

When used in cosmetics, exempt colors still must comply with all the specifications, uses, restrictions and labeling requirements stated in the regulations.

Straight Color

A "straight color" refers to any color additive listed in the Code of Federal Regulations.

Lake

A "lake" is a straight color that has been modified at a chemical level (not by just mixing them up with something else). In some cases, special restrictions apply to their use.

Intended Use

It doesn't matter whether or not a color is certified or not, it can still only be used for the approved uses.

See Appendix A for a complete list of all approved color additives as of the date of this publication.

Cosmetics Generally

A color additive that is approved for "cosmetics generally" may be used in any cosmetic, including lip products, but not in the eye area unless it is specifically approved for eye area use as well.

Eye-Area Use

A color additive may only be used in the eye area if the regulations specifically permit it. The eye area includes the eyebrow, skin below the eyebrow, eyelids, eyelashes and the area just below the lower eyelashes.

Externally Applied Cosmetics

"Externally applied" means applied to the outside of the body. It does not apply to the lips or any body surface covered by mucous membrane (which includes, for example, the lips, nostrils, ears and genital area).

In other words, a color additive that is approved for external use may not be used in products that are applied to the lips or any body surface covered by mucous membrane unless specifically approved for that use.

Bath Products

As noted above, color additives that are approved for external application may not be used in products that are applied to mucous membranes.

The FDA has determined that color additives that are approved for external application may be used in in-bath products because of the limited potential of exposure to the color additive[1].

Therefore, cosmetics intended for in-bath use may include color additives that are approved for general use or external application in cosmetics in amounts consistent with current good manufacturing practice (unless the regulations provide additional limitations).

---

[1] In early 2007 there was conflicting information on the FDA website about which color additives could be used in bubble bath products. The author queried the FDA and received the information included here as their official determination on the subject. The FDA website was subsequently corrected.

Chapter 14
Special Cases

Tamper Evident Packaging

Liquid oral hygiene products (e.g., mouthwashes, fresheners) and all cosmetic vaginal products (e.g., douches, tablets) must be packaged in tamper-resistant packages when sold at retail.

To be tamper resistant a package must have a way to alert a consumer if the package has been tampered with. For example, it could be a shrink or tape seal or a sealed carton, tube or pouch which obviously shows when it has been previously opened.

The design (i.e. breakable cap or blister pack) or appearance (i.e. logo, vignette, other illustration) must be made so that it can't be substituted or replaced if the package has been opened.

The tamper-resistant feature may be on the immediate or outer container or both. The package must also bear a prominently placed statement alerting the consumer to the tamper-resistant feature. This statement must remain unaffected if the tamper-resistant feature is breached or missing.

For example, the labeling statement on a bottle with a shrink band could say "For your protection, this bottle has an imprinted seal around the neck."

Animal Grooming Products

The FDA cosmetic rules do not apply to products intended for use on animals. Companies that make dog shampoo or cream rinse, hoof cream, horse sparkle make-up or poodle hair dye are not required to list the ingredients on their packaging or otherwise comply with FDA cosmetic labeling regulations.

However, if the products are **also** intended for use on humans (i.e. "hoof cream" that can also be used on human fingernails) then the FDA does have jurisdiction and the product must follow and comply with all cosmetic labeling ingredients.

Remember that the FDA looks at the intended use of a product, which is determined by what the labeling of the product says. The "labeling" includes all labels and other written, printed or graphic matter on or accompanying the product — labels, inserts, risers, display packs, leaflets, promotional literature or any other written or printed information distributed with a product, including statements made on a website to describe or promote the product.

Let's say you are selling a "mane and tail shampoo" that is supposedly for horses and you even state "for horses" right on the product label. If you say "can also be used by humans" or "gives great shine to your hair" or any other statement that implies it's recommended or intended to be used by a person anywhere in the accompanying materials, display, or website, then it is a cosmetic and must be labeled accordingly.

Aromatherapy

Aromatherapy products fall into something of a grey area. The guiding determination is again the intended use, which is ultimately determined by how the consumer views the product based on the product label and accompanying promotional materials.

Cosmetic Aromatherapy Product

A product intended to be used on the body and scented with a blend of essential oils that smells really good and is promoted to <u>make the person feel more attractive</u> would be a **cosmetic**. The exact essential oil ingredients could be included in the ingredients list OR they could be grouped under the heading of "fragrance" and not individually listed. (See ingredient listing specifications in Section 2.)

Home Environment Products

A home environment product (candle, room spray, diffuser, etc.) scented with a blend of essential oils that smells really good and is promoted to <u>improve the environment</u> (by making it smell nice) is **neither a cosmetic nor drug** and does not fall within the FDA regulations for labeling.

There is no requirement that the ingredients are listed on the product; whether the essential oils used are listed or promoted is optional.

Home environment products ARE consumer commodities, so they still require the identity of the item, the name and address of the manufacturer and the net contents on the package in accordance with the FPLA.

Drug Aromatherapy Product

Alternatively, a product made of a blend of essential oils that smells really good and is promoted to make the person <u>sleep better"</u> or <u>help relieve the tension of quitting smoking</u> would be a **drug** because it is promoted to affect the body's structure or function. It doesn't matter if the product is applied to the body or the home environment.

As a drug it requires approval by the FDA before being put on the market.

Once again, the determining factor on what regulation(s) apply is the **intended use** of the product, as perceived by the consumer based on the product label and accompanying promotional materials.

Anti-Microbial or Anti-Bacterial

Products which specifically claim to be anti-microbial or anti-bacterial are classed as drugs and must be labeled as such.

Sunscreens

Claiming a product is a "sunscreen" or using similar sun protection terminology in a product's labeling generally classes the product as a drug. That is because the active ingredients making the product a sunscreen work by affecting the structure or function to change the normal physiological response to solar radiation.

In some cases a sunscreen ingredient might be used in a product for non-therapeutic, non-physiological uses (for example, as a color additive or to protect the color of the product). To avoid consumer misunderstanding, if a cosmetic product contains a sunscreen ingredient **and** uses the term "sunscreen" or similar sun protection terminology anywhere in its labeling, the term must be qualified by explaining the benefit to the cosmetic product provided by the sunscreen ingredient (for example, "Contains a sunscreen to protect product color."). Otherwise, the product may be subject to regulation as a drug.

"Naked" Products

The FDA regulations specifically apply to products that are traveling through interstate commerce. Therefore, any product that is shipped must be appropriately labeled.

When products are shipped without retail or consumer labels because the cosmetic is going to be processed, labeled or repacked at a different establishment, some different rules apply.

Sending To A Different Facility

If the person who ships the product is the same person who receives it (i.e. sending to another facility owned by the same person or company), then the product is exempt from labeling requirements.

Sending To Another Person (Private Label)

If the products are being sent to someone else (a customer) with the understanding that the customer will be labeling the product, then there must be a written agreement signed by both parties. The agreement must contain specific directions for the processing, labeling or repacking that, if followed, will insure that the product will not be adulterated or misbranded. Both parties must keep a signed copy of the agreement on file for 2 years.

In other words, if you are going to ship a case of unlabeled products to a customer with the understanding that the customer will label them, then you must have a written agreement that:

a) is signed by both you and the customer;

b) includes the postal addresses of both you and the customer;

c) contains accurate specifications for labeling the product, which would include the ingredients list, any necessary warning statements, accurate weight and directions as to any other statements required on the label.

d) both parties keep on file for 2 years.

The exemption becomes void from the beginning if the products are adulterated when they are unpacked or if the sender refuses to provide a copy of the agreement when requested.

Note: Being exempted by the FDA from the labeling requirements for the individual products does NOT exempt the case-pack labeling required by the FTC or any state agencies. If "naked" products are packed within a case-pack, the outside the the case-pack should include:

a) name of the product

b) identity

c) quantity of contents (see Chapter 6).

Chapter 15
Supplier Responsibilities

All cosmetic ingredient labeling depends on a correct statement of what is in the product. Since most people who make soap and cosmetics don't make all their own ingredients, they must rely upon their suppliers to provide the necessary information to correctly label the finished cosmetic product.

As a result, every supplier has a responsibility to provide information about the ingredients they sell that is accurate and sufficient to enable legal and correct labeling of the finished cosmetic product. A supplier who cannot or refuses to provide the necessary information makes it impossible to follow the labeling regulations for any finished product that uses that ingredient and creates a legal and ethical liability for the person trying to sell the final cosmetic product.

If a supplier is unwilling or unable to provide you with the information you need to follow the law, consider finding a new supplier.

Cosmetic Raw Material

A Cosmetic raw material is:

> *Any ingredient, including an ingredient that is a mixture, which is used in the manufacture of a cosmetic product for commercial distribution and is supplied to a cosmetic product manufacturer, packer, or distributor by a cosmetic raw material manufacturer or supplier.*

Cosmetic raw materials by law are also considered cosmetics and must follow the labeling rules for cosmetics.

That means the package containing the ingredient must have the following information:

Principal Display Panel

a) Name of the Product

b) Identity of Product

c) Unsubstantiated Safety Warning (if required)

d) Net Quantity of Contents

Information Panels

a) Directions for Safe Use

b) Warnings (if required)

c) Name and Place of Business

d) Ingredient Declaration

e) Any Other Required Information

Ingredient Listing

As noted above, the package label must list the ingredient(s) in the raw cosmetic material. The ingredient(s) must be listed in the correct format (i.e. the INCI name based on the 2nd to current edition of the *Cosmetic Ingredient Dictionary*) and in accordance with all regulations on the ingredient declaration.

Mixture of Ingredients

When using a raw cosmetic material that is made up of a mixture of ingredients, it is often necessary to know the percentages of the individual constituents in order to place them correctly in the ingredient declaration of the finished product.

A supplier should either provide the actual percentages of the ingredients in the raw cosmetic material or be willing to assist in creating a correct ingredient list.

If a supplier won't give you the necessary information, you are at risk of selling a misbranded (and therefore illegal) product.

Example - Using a Lotion Base

You purchase a lotion base from a supplier. If you add color at 1% and fragrance a 2.5%, you must determine where to put those in the ingredient declaration for the final product.

The supplier should either:

1) provide you with the percentages for enough of the lotion base ingredients to enable you to determine where 1% and 2.5% would go in the descending order of predominance, or

2) Tell you where to place the 1% and 2.5% ingredients within the ingredient listing (if they are unwilling to tell you the percentages of all the ingredients in the product).

Example - Using an Oil Blend

You purchase a unique oil blend from a supplier. For this example, let's say the oil blend is made up of coconut oil (75%), sunflower oil (20%) and shea butter (5%).

If you use the oil blend to make a lotion bar, then the formula might be: oil blend 90%, cocoa butter 8%, fragrance 2%. In that case, the ingredient listing would be:

Ingredients: Coconut oil, sunflower oil, cocoa butter, shea butter, and fragrance.

If you use the oil bend to make soap, then the formula might be: oil blend (65%), water (22%), sodium hydroxide (9%), fragrance (3%), purple ultramarine (1%) [1] In that case, the ingredient listing would be:

Ingredients: Coconut oil, water, sodium hydroxide, sunflower oil, shea butter, fragrance and purple ultra-marine.

---

[1] Note this is NOT a valid soap recipe.

Obviously, the percentages in the oil blend must be known in order to correctly label the finished product.

Calculating the Percentage in the Final Product

To calculate the amount of each ingredient of a raw cosmetic material in the finished product, the formula is:

$$% \text{ of raw cosmetic material used}$$
$$\times \quad % \text{ of the ingredient in the raw cosmetic material}$$
$$= \quad % \text{ in final product}$$

Example of Calculating Percentages

(Using the example of the oil blend in soap from above.)

$$65% \text{ oil blend used}$$
$$\times \quad 20% \text{ sunflower oil in oil blend}$$
$$= \quad 13% \text{ sunflower oil in final product}$$

Using "(and)" in the Ingredient List

It is never acceptable to use "(and)" in the ingredient list. That is a food labeling option and does not apply to cosmetics.

Incorrect Ingredient Declaration

Using the above soap example, the following ingredient declaration is incorrect and would render the product misbranded (and in non-compliance with the law):

Ingredients: Oil blend (coconut oil (and) sunflower oil (and) shea butter), water, sodium hydroxide, fragrance and purple ultramarine.

Summary

In short, when selling raw cosmetic ingredients it is the supplier's responsibility to provide customers with sufficient information to properly use the ingredient and correctly label the finished cosmetic product(s) that contain the ingredient.

Section 4

Appendix

Appendix A
Color Additives

Colors Exempt From Certification

Color	Uses and Restrictions
Annatto	Cosmetics generally including eye area use.
Caramel	Cosmetics generally including eye area use.
Carmine	Cosmetics generally including eye area use.
beta-Carotene	Cosmetics generally including eye area use.
Bismuth citrate(3)	Cosmetics intended for coloring hair on the scalp only, NTE 0.1 percent in combination with a list of substances.
Disodium EDTA-copper	Coloring of shampoos that are cosmetics.
Potassium sodium copper chlorophyllin (Chlorophyllin copper complex)	Coloring dentifrices that are cosmetics (w/ restrictions).
Dihydroxyacetone	Externally applied cosmetics intended solely or in part to impart color to the human body.
Bismuth oxychloride	Cosmetics generally including eye area use.
Guaiazulene	Externally applied cosmetics.
Henna(3)	Coloring hair but not for eye lashes, eyebrows, or eye area.
Iron oxides	Cosmetics generally including eye area use.
Ferric ammonium ferrocyanide	Externally applied cosmetics including eye area use.
Ferric ferrocyanide	Externally applied cosmetics including eye area use.
Chromium hydroxide green	Externally applied cosmetics including eye area use.
Chromium oxide greens	Externally applied cosmetics including eye area use.
Guanine	Cosmetics generally including eye area use.

Lead acetate(3)	Cosmetics intended for coloring hair on the scalp only, NTE 0.6 percent (weight/volume).
Pyrophyllite	Externally applied cosmetics.
Mica	Cosmetics generally including eye area use.
Silver (3)	Coloring fingernail polish, NTE 1% of final product.
Titanium dioxide	Cosmetics including eye area use.
Aluminum powder	Externally applied cosmetics including eye area use.
Bronze powder	Cosmetics generally including eye area use.
Copper powder	Cosmetics generally including eye area use.
Ultramarines	Externally applied cosmetics including eye area use.
Manganese violet	Cosmetics generally including eye area use.
Zinc oxide	Cosmetics including eye area use.
Luminescent zinc sulfide (3)	Nail polish and externally applied facial makeup, NTE 10% of final product for limited, occasional use. Special labeling requirements.

NTE means "not to exceed".

Certifiable Colors

Certifiable colors may be listed on the ingredients list as just the color and number (i.e. "Blue 1")

Color	Uses and Restrictions
D&C Black No. 2(3)	Eyeliner, brush-on-brow, eye shadow, mascara, lipstick, blushers and rouge, makeup and foundation, and nail enamel.
FD&C Blue No. 1	Cosmetics generally. Eye area use (includes lake)
D&C Blue No. 4	Externally applied cosmetics.
D&C Brown No. 1	Externally applied cosmetics.
FD&C Green No. 3	Cosmetics generally.
D&C Green No. 5	Cosmetics generally. Eye area use.
D&C Green No. 6	Externally applied cosmetics.
D&C Green No. 8	Externally applied cosmetics (NTE 0.01% (by wt) of finished cosmetic product).
D&C Orange No. 4	Externally applied cosmetics.
D&C Orange No. 5	Externally applied cosmetics. Mouthwashes, dentifrices, lipsticks, and other lip cosmetics, NTE 5 percent.

D&C Orange No. 10	Externally applied cosmetics.
D&C Orange No. 11	Externally applied cosmetics.
FD&C Red No. 4	Externally applied cosmetics.
D&C Red No. 6	Cosmetics generally.
D&C Red No. 7	Cosmetics generally.
D&C Red No. 17	Externally applied cosmetics.
D&C Red No. 21	Cosmetics generally.
D&C Red No. 22	Cosmetics generally.
D&C Red No. 27	Cosmetics generally.
D&C Red No. 28	Cosmetics generally.
D&C Red No. 30	Cosmetics generally.
D&C Red No. 31	Externally applied cosmetics.
D&C Red No. 33	Externally applied cosmetics; mouthwashes, dentifrices; cosmetic lip products (NTE 3% (by wt) of finished cosmetic product).
D&C Red No. 34	Externally applied cosmetics.
D&C Red No. 36	Externally applied cosmetics; cosmetic lip products (NTE 3% (by wt) of finished cosmetic product).
FD&C Red No. 40(3)	Cosmetics generally. Eye area use (includes Al lake). No oxidizing or reducing agents that may affect integrity
D&C Violet No. 2	Externally applied cosmetics.
Ext. D&C Violet No. 2	Externally applied cosmetics.
FD&C Yellow No. 5	Cosmetics generally. Eye area use (includes Aluminum lake)
FD&C Yellow No. 6	Cosmetics generally.
D&C Yellow No. 7	Externally applied cosmetics.
Ext. D&C Yellow No. 7	Externally applied cosmetics.
D&C Yellow No. 8	Externally applied cosmetics.
D&C Yellow No. 10	Cosmetics generally.
D&C Yellow No. 11	Externally applied cosmetics.

Appendix B
INCI Names

INCI is an acronym for International Nomenclature of Cosmetic Ingredients. It's the term that we use to say that the name for an ingredient is "standard".

Actually, there are several standards for cosmetic ingredient names. The most common, and most generally referred to is the International Cosmetic Ingredient Dictionary, published by the *Cosmetic, Toiletry and Fragrance Association* (recently renamed the *Personal Care Council*). As of the date of publication of this book, the most recent edition of the dictionary is the 11th edition.

Chemicals and derived substances are fairly straightforward in how they should be named and listed. When a new product is created, the manufacturer submits it CTFA. CTFA approves a standardized name and it is added to the ingredient dictionary.

When you purchase a chemical-type ingredient, your supplier should provide you with the correct term to use on the ingredient listing.

INCI Listing

Following is a list of some of the more commonly used ingredients in handcrafted soaps and cosmetics, listed by the common name. It is not a complete list.

While this list is reasonably accurate, you should with your supplier to verify the exact INCI name for particular ingredient. This is especially important with plant-based ingredients as sometimes there are several sub-species, each with a different name, so you need to make sure you have the right one.

Soap

As a note, "saponified oil of ____" or "saponified ____ oil" are not standard INCI names and are not included in any edition of the *International Cosmetic Ingredient Dictionary.* The correct format is the chemical name of the resultant soap based on the type of oil and type of lye used (i.e. "sodium palmate" or "postassium cocoate")

See Chapter 9 for additional information on ingredient listings for soap.

Botanicals

Botanicals include any plant-based ingredient. The list below shows the latin name for common botanical ingredients. The "correct" way to list botanicals has changed over the years, so you have several correct options to choose from. See Chapter 7 for additional information on the different formats and determining which one(s) to use.

* An asterisk by the common name indicates that the essential oil of the plant is listed in the FDA regulations as "Generally regarded as safe".

Alfalfa *	Medicago sativa
Alkanet Root	Alkanna tinctoria
Allantoin	Allantoin
Allspice *	Pimenta officinalis
Almond Oil, Sweet	Prunus amygdalus dulcis
Almond, bitter (free from prussic acid) *	Prunus amygdalus Prunus armeniaca Prunus persica
Aloe Vera	Aloe barbadensis
Ambrette (seed) *	Hibiscus moschatus
Angelica root, seed or stem *	Angelica archangelica
Angostura (cusparia bark) *	Galipea officinalis
Anise *	Pimpinella anisum
Apricot Kernel	Prunus armeniaca

Apricot Seed	Prunus armeniaca
Arrowroot	Maranta arundinacea
Ascorbic Acid	Ascorbic Acid
Atlas Cedarwood Oil	Cedrus atlantica
Avocadol	Persea gratissima
Babassul	Orbignya oleifera
Baking Soda	Sodium Bicarbonate
Balm (lemon balm) *	Melissa officinalis
Balsam of Peru *	Myroxylon pereirae
Basil *	Ocimum basilicum
Bay (myrcia oil) *	Pimenta racemosa
Bay leaves *	Laurus nobilis
Beef Tallow	Tallow
Beer	Beer
Beeswax	Cera alba or Beeswax
Beet Powder	Beta Vulgaris
Bentonite Clay	Bentonite
Benzaldehyde	Benzaldehyde or Fragrance or Flavor
Bergamot *	Citrus aurantium
BHT	BHT
Bitter Orange	Citrus aurantium amara
Blackcurrant	Ribes nigrum
Blackthorn (berries) *	Prunus spinosa
Bladderwrack	Fucus nesiculosus
Blood Orange	Citrus aurantium dulcis
Bois de rose *	Aniba rosaeodora
Borage	Borago officinalis
Borax	Borax
Butter	Butter
Buttermilk	Buttermilk
Cacao *	Theobroma cacao
Cajeput	Melaleuca leucadendron cajaputi
Calamine	Calamine
Calcium Carbonate	Calcium Carbonate
Calendula	Calendula officinalis

Cananga *	Cananga odorata
Candelilla Wax	Euphorbia cerifera (Candelilla) wax
Canola	Brassica napus
Capsicum *	Capsicum frutescens Capsicum annuum
Caraway *	Carum carvi
Carbomer	Carbomer
Cardamom (seed) *	Elettaria cardamomum
Carnauba Wax	Copernicia cerifera
Carob bean *	Ceratonia siliqua
Carrot *	Daucus carota
Cascarilla bark *	Croton eluteria
Cassia bark, Chinese *	Cinnamomum cassia
Cassia bark, Padang or Batavia*	Cinnamomum burmanni
Cassia bark, Saigon *	Cinnamomum loureirii
Castor Oil	Ricinus communis (Castor) seed oil
Catnip	Nepeta cataria
Celery (seed) *	Apium graveolens
Cetyl Alcohol	Cetyl Alcohol
Chamomile, Hungarian *	Matricaria chamomilla
Chamomile, Roman or English *	Anthemis nobilis
Cherry, wild, bark *	Prunus serotina
Chervil *	Anthriscus cerefolium
Chicory *	Cichorium intybus
Chlorophyll	Chlorophyll
Cinnamon bark, Ceylon *	Cinnamomum zeylanicum
Cinnamon bark, Chinese *	Cinnamomum cassia
Cinnamon bark, Saigon *	Cinnamomum loureirii
Cinnamon leaf, Ceylon *	Cinnamomum zeylanicum
Cinnamon leaf, Chinese *	Cinnamomum cassia
Cinnamon leaf, Saigon *	Cinnamomum loureirii
Citric Acid	Citric Acid
Citronella *	Cymbopogon nardus
Clary (clary sage) *	Salvia sclarea
Clay, China	Kaolin
Clay, Red	Montmorillonite
Clay, White Kaolin	Kaolin
Clay, Bentonite	Bentonite

Clove bud, stem, leaf *	Eugenia caryophyllata
Clover *	Trifolium
Coca (decocainized) *	Erythroxylum coca
Cocoa Butter	Theobroma cacao (Cocoa) seed butter
Coconut Oil	Cocos nucifera (Coconut) oil
Coffee *	Coffea
Cola nut *	Cola acuminata
Comfrey	Symphytum officinale
Coriander *	Coriandrum sativum
Corn (starch, silk, meal) *	Zea mays
Cream	Cream
Cumin *	Cuminum cyminum
Cusparia bark *	Galipea officinalis
Cypress Oil	Cupressus sempervirens
Dandelion (leaf, root) *	Taraxacum officinale
Denatured Alcohol	SD Alcohol
Dill *	Anethum graveolens
Dipropylene Glycol	Dipropylene Glycol
Dog grass (quackgrass, triticum) *	Agropyron repens
DPG USP	Dipropylene Glycol
Dulse	Palmaria Palmata
EDTA; Tetrasodium	Tetrasodium EDTA
Elder flowers *	Sambucus canadensis
Emu Oil	Emu Oil
Emulsifying Wax NF	Emulsifying Wax NF
Epsom Salt	Magnesium Sulfate
Estragole (esdragol, esdragon, tarragon) *	Artemisia dracunculus
Estragon (tarragon) *	Artemisia dracunculus
Eucalyptus	Eucalyptus citriodora Eucalyptus globulus Eucalyptus radiata Eucalyptus smithii
Evening Primrose	Oenothera biennis
Fennel, sweet *	Foeniculum vulgare
Fenugreek *	Trigonella foenum-graecum
Fir Needle	Abies Sibirica
Flax Oil	Linum usitatissmum (Flax) seed oil

Fractionated Coconut Oil	Caprylic/Capric Triglyceride
Frankincense Oil	Olibanum
Galanga (galangal) *	Alpinia officinarum
Galbanum Oil	Ferula galbaniflua (Galbanum) resin oil
Garlic *	Allium sativum
Geranium Oil	Pelargonium graveolens
Geranium, East Indian *	Cymbopogon martini
Geranium, rose *	Pelargonium graveolens
Ginger *	Zingiber officinale
Glycerine	Glycerine
Glyceryl Monosteareate SE	Glyceryl Stearate
Glycyrrhiza *	Glycyrrhiza glabra
Grape Seed Oil	Vitis Vinifera (Grape) Seed Oil
Grapefruit *	Citrus paradisi Citrus grandis
Green Tea	Camellia Sinensis
Guar Gum	Cyamopsis tetragonoloba (Guar) gum
Guava *	Psidium
Hazel Nut Oil	Corylus americana Corylus avellana
Helichrysum Oil	Helichrysum italicum
Hemp Oil	Cannabis sativa (Hemp) seed oil
Hickory bark *	Carya spp.
Honey	Honey
Hops *	Humulus lupulus
Horehound (hoarhound) *	Marrubium vulgare
Horsemint *	Monarda punctata
Hyssop *	Hyssopus officinalis
Iron Oxide (all)	Iron Oxides
Jasmine *	Jaminum officinale
Jojoba Oil	Simmondsia chinensis (Jojoba) seed oil
Juniper (berries) *	Juniperus communis
Kaolin	Kaolin
Kokum Butter	Garcinia indica seed bButter
Kola nut *	Cola acuminata Schott
Kukui Nut Oil	Aleurites moluccana (Kukui Nut) seed oil
Lactose	Lactose
Lanolin	Lanolin

Lanolin	Lanolin
Lard	Lard
Laurel berries *	Laurus nobilis
Lavandin *	Lavandula hybrida
Lavender	Lavandula angustifolia
Lavender; Spike *	Lavandula spica Lavandula latifolia
Lecithin	Lecithin
Lemon *	Citrus limon
Lemon grass *	Cymbopogon citratus Cymbopogon schoenanthus
Lemon peel *	Citrus limon
Licorice *	Glycyrrhiza glabra
Lime *	Citrus aurantifolia
Linden flowers *	Tilia spp.
Linseed	Linum usitatissmum (Linseed) seed oil
Locust bean *	Ceratonia siliqua.
Lupulin *	Humulus lupulus
Macadamia Nut Oil	Macadamia ternifolia seed oil
Mace *	Myristica fragrans
Magnesium Carbonate	Magnesium Carbonate
Malt (extract) *	Hordeum vulgare
Mandarin *	Citrus reticulata
Mango Butter	Mangifera Indica (Mango Butter) Seed Oil
Marjoram, sweet *	Majorana hortensis
Marshmallow Root Powder	Althea offinalis root
Meadowfoam Oil	Limnanthes alba (Meadowfoam) seed oil
Melissa	Melissa officinalis
Menthol Crystals	Menthol
Mica	Mica
Mineral Oil	Paraffinum Liquidum
Molasses (extract) *	Saccharum officinarum
MSM	Dimethyl Sulfone
Mugwort	Artemisia vulgaris
Mustard *	Brassica
Myrrh Oil	Commiphora myrrha (Myrrh) oil
Myrtle Oil	Myrtus communis (Myrtle) oil
Naringin *	Citrus paradisi

Neem Oil	Azadirachta indica (Neem) oil
Neroli, bigarade *	Citrus aurantium
Nettles Leaf Powder	Urtica Dioica
Niaouli Oil	Melaleuca leucadendron viridiflora (Niaouli) oil
Nutmeg *	Myristica fragrans
Oat (flower, meal, powder)	Avena sativa
Olive Oil	Olea europaea (Olive) oil
Onion *	Allium cepa
Orange, Bitter	Citrus aurantium amara
Oregano	Oreganum vulgare
Origanum *	Origanum
Palm Oil	Elaeis guineensis (Palm) oil
Palmarosa *	Cymbopogon martini
Paprika *	Capsicum annuum
Parsley *	Petroselinum crispum
Patchouli Oil	Pogostemon Cablin Oil
Peach Kernel Oil	Prunus persica (Peach) kernel oil
Peanut Oil	Arachis hypogaea (Peanut) oil
Pepper, black *	Piper nigrum L.
Pepper, white *	Piper nigrum L.
Peppermint *	Mentha piperita
Peruvian balsam *	Myroxylon pereirae
Petitgrain *	Citrus aurantium
Petitgrain lemon *	Citrus limon
Petitgrain mandarin or tangerine *	Citrus reticulata
Pimenta *	Pimenta officinalis
Pipsissewa leaves *	Chimaphila umbellata
Pomegranate *	Punica granatum
Poppyseed	Papaver somniferum
Potassium Sorbate	Potassium Sorbate
Potato	Solanum tuberosum
Prickly ash bark *	Xanthoxylum (or Zanthoxylum) Americanum
Propylene Glycol	Propylene Glycol
Pumice	Pumice
Pumpkin Seed Oil	Cucurbita pepo (Pumpkin) seed oil
Rapeseed Oil	Brassica campestris (Rapeseed) seed oil
Red Turkey Oil	Sulfated ricinus communis (Castor) oil

Rice (Oil, starch, flour, powder)	Oryza sativa
Rose (absolute, otto of roses, attar of roses, buds, flowers, petals, fruit (hips), leaves) *	Rosa alba Rosa centifolia Rosa damascena Rosa gallica and other varieties (check with your supplier)
Rose geranium *	Pelargonium graveolens
Rosehip Oil	Rosa Mosqueta (Rosehip) Fruit Oil
Rosemary *	Rosmarinus officinalis
Rosewood Oil	Aniba rosaeodora (Rosewood) wood oil
Royal Jelly	Royal Jelly
Rue *	Ruta graveolens
Safflower Oil	Carthamus tinctorius (Safflower) seed oil
Saffron *	Crocus sativus
Sage *	Salvia officinalis
Sage, Greek *	Salvia triloba
Sage, Spanish *	Salvia lavandulaefolia
Salt	Sodium Chloride
Sandalwood Oil	Santalum album
Savory, summer *	Satureia hortensis
Savory, winter *	Satureia montana
Schinus molle *	Schinus molle
Sea Buckthorn	Hippophae rhamnoides
Sesame	Sesamum indicum
Shea Butter	Butyrospermum parkii (Shea Butter) fruit
Sloe (berries) *	Prunus spinosa
Soybean Oil	Glycine soja (Soybean) oil
Spearmint *	Mentha spicata
St. John's Wort Oil	Hypericum perforatum oil
Stearic Acid	Stearic Acid
Stevia	Eupatorium rebaudianum bertoni
Sugar	Sucrose
Sugar, Brown / White	Sucrose
Sunflower Oil	Helianthus annuus (Sunflower) seed oil
Sweet Fennel Oil	Foeniculum vulgare
Sweet Marjoram Oil	Origanum majorana
Talc	Talc
Tallow	Tallow

Tamarind *	Tamarindus indica
Tangerine *	Citrus reticulata
Tarragon *	Artemisia dracunculus
Tea *	Thea sinensis.
TEA	Triethanolamine
Tea Tree Oil	Melaleuca alternifolia
Thyme *	Thymus vulgaris Thymus zygis
Thyme, wild or creeping *	Thymus serpyllum
Titanium Dioxide	Titanium Dioxide
Tomato	Solanum tycopersicum
Tuberose *	Polianthes tuberosa
Turmeric *	Curcuma longa L.
Valerian Root	Valeriana officinalis
Vanilla *	Vanilla planifolia
Vetiver Oil	Vetivera zizanoides
Violet (flowers, leaves) *	Viola odorata
Vitamin E	Tocopherol
Vitamin E Acetate	Tocopheryl Acetate
Walnut	Juglans regia
Wheat Germ	Triticum vulgare germ
White Camphor	Cinnamomum camphora
Wild cherry bark *	Prunus serotina
Witchhazel	Hamamelis virginiana distillate
Xanthan Gum	Xanthan Gum
Ylang-ylang *	Cananga odorata
Yogurt	yogurt
Zedoary bark	Curcuma zedoaria Rosc.
Zinc Oxide	Zinc Oxide

Appendix C
Prohibited & Restricted Ingredients

Generally, an ingredient being used in a cosmetic does not need to be pre-approved before being used. That means a manufacturer may use any ingredient in the formulation of a cosmetic product provided that the ingredient and the finished cosmetic are safe, the product is properly labeled, and the use of the specific substance is not otherwise disallowed.

There are, however, a few of exceptions.

Unsubstantiated Safety

If there are untested ingredients or ingredient combinations used, or if the safety of the cosmetic cannot be adequately substantiated, then product label must include a warning statement on the Primary Display Panel:

> **Warning: The safety of this product has not been determined.**

See Chapter 11, Warnings, for more information on when this warning label should be used.

Color Additives

The use of **all** color additives is regulated by the FDA. Only approved color additives may be used in cosmetics, and then only for the very specific use for which they are authorized.

See Chapter 12 for information on color additives and Appendix A for a list of approved color additives.

Prohibited Ingredients

Some ingredients are completely prohibited for use in cosmetic products. It's unlikely that you would ever use these ingredients, but they are, just in case:

Bithionol
> May cause photo-contact sensitization

Chlorofluorocarbon propellants

Chloroform
> Animal carcinogenicity and likely hazard to human health. Residual amounts from its use as a processing solvent during manufacture, or as a by-product from the synthesis of an ingredient are excepted.

Halogenated salicylanilides
> **(di-, tri-, metabromsalan and tetrachlorosalicylanilide)**
> May cause photocontact sensitization.

Methylene chloride
> Animal carcinogenicity and likely hazard to human health.

Vinyl chloride
> Carcinogen.

Zirconium-containing complexe
> Prohibited in aerosol cosmetic products because of their toxic effect on lungs, including the formation of granulomas.

Prohibited cattle materials
> To protect against bovine spongiform encephalopathy (BSE), also known as "mad cow disease," cosmetics may not be manufactured from, processed with, or otherwise contain, prohibited cattle materials. This does not include tallow that contains no more than 0.15 percent insoluble impurities, tallow derivatives, and hides and hide-derived products, and milk and milk products.

Soap made by saponifying tallow is considered a "tallow derivative". However, if you are using tallow in your soap, it would be wise to check with your supplier to ensure that the tallow contains no more than .15% insoluble impurities and is rendered in accordance with the FDA regulations.

Restricted Ingredients

Some ingredients are allowed, but restricted. In the very unlikely chance that you are going to use any of these restricted ingredients, check the FDA website (along with an experienced chemist and a good lawyer) beforehand.

Hexachlorophene

Mercury compounds

Sunscreens in cosmetics (generally classed as a drug)

Appendix D
Metric Conversions

Weight (Mass)

1 ounce	=	28.349	g
1 pound	=	453.592	g
		0.45359	kg
1 grain	=	64.7989	mg
1 milligram	=	.00003527	oz
		.0154332	grain
1 gram	=	.03527	oz
1 kilogram	=	2.2046	lb

Length

1 inch	=	2.54	cm
1 foot	=	30.48	cm
1 yard	=	0.914	m
1 rod	=	5.0292	m
1 millimeter	=	0.03937	in
1 centimeter	=	0.3937	in
1 meter	=	3.2808	ft

Volume or Capacity

1 fluid ounce	=	29.5735	mL
1 liquid pint	=	473.177	mL
		0.473177	L
1 liquid quart	=	946.353	mL
		0.946353	L
1 gallon	=	3.7854	L
1 bushel	=	35.239	L
1 dry pint	=	550.6105	mL
		0.55061	L
1 dry quart	=	1.10122	L
1 peck	=	8.809768	L
1 gill	=	18.294	mL
1 milliliter	=	0.033814	fl oz
1 liter	=	1.05669	liq qt
		0.26417	gal
1 cubic inch	=	16.3871	cm^3
1 cubic foot	=	0.028316	m^3
		28.3168	L
1 cubic yard	=	0.764555	m^3
1 cubic centimeter	=	0.0610237	in^3
1 cubic decimeter	=	0.0353147	ft^3
1 cubic meter	=	35.3147	ft^3
		1.20795	yd^3

Area

1 square inch	=	6.5416	cm²
1 square foot	=	929.03	cm²
1 square yard	=	0.836127	m²
1 square centimeter	=	0.155	in²
1 square decimeter	=	0.107639	ft²
1 square meter	=	10.7639	ft²

Metric Conversions
Examples of Rounding

Weight

to convert ounces to grams - multiply ounces x 28.3495 grams

Inch/Pound	Calculated SI	Rounded SI
1.0 oz	28.3495 g	28 g
5.0 oz	141.747 g	142 g
10 1/4 oz	290.582 g	291 g
16.0 oz	453.5924 g	454 g
32 oz	907.184 g	907 g
48 oz	1360.776 g	1.36 kg
5 lb	2.26796185 kg	2.27 kg
10 lb	4.5359237 kg	4.54 kg
25 lb	11.33980925 kg	11.3 kg

Liquid Volume

to convert fluid ounces to milliliters multiply fluid ounces x 29.5735 milliliters.

Inch/Pound	Calculated SI	Rounded SI
1 fl oz	29.5735 mL	30 mL
8 fl oz	236.588 mL	237 mL
16 fl oz	473.176 mL	473 mL
32 fl oz	946.353 mL	946 mL
1 gal	3.78541 L	3.79 L
5 gal	18.92705 L	18.9 L

Length

to convert inches to millimeters multiply inches x 24.5 millimeters

Inch/Pound	Calculated SI	Rounded SI
1 in	25.4 mm	25 mm
10.5 in	266.7 mm	267 mm or 26.7 cm
1 ft	30.48 cm	305 mm or 30.5 cm
5 ft	152.4 cm	152 cm or 1.5 m
50 ft	15.24003 m	15.2 m
100 ft	30.48006 m	30.5 m

Appendix E
State Authorities

All US states were searched for information pertinent to the manufacture and labeling of handcrafted soaps, cosmetics and other products. Where information was found, a brief summary is given along with where you can find additional data.

The contact information provided is that of the agency governing cosmetics or, if there is not a particular state agency, then the part of the state government dealing with businesses in general is noted.

ALABAMA
Alabama Department of Agriculture & Industries
1445 Federal Drive, Montgomery, AL 36107
1-800-642-7761   www.alabama.gov

The Alabama Department of Agriculture and Industries document "Agricultural Commodities Inspection Administrative Code, Chapter 80-1-22: Foods, Drugs and Cosmetics" includes state laws and regulations regarding labeling.
See: www.alabamaadministrativecode.state.al.us/docs/agr/1AGR22.htm

ALASKA
Alaska Corporations, Business & Professional Licenses
P.O. Box 110808, Juneau, AK 99811-0808
Tel: (907)465-2550   Fax: (907)465-2974
www.state.ak.us

The Alaska Food, Drug and Cosmetic Act can be found at:
http://touchngo.com/lglcntr/akstats/Statutes/Title17/Chapter20.htm

ARIZONA

Arizona Department of Commerce

1700 W. Washington, Suite 600, Phoenix, Arizona 85007

Tel: (602)771-1100

www.az.gov

ARKANSAS

Arkansas Division of Health

P.O. Box 1437, Little Rock, AR 72203

1-800-482-8988

www.arkansas.gov

Access the "Arkansas Food, Drug and Cosmetic Act" online. Its topics include advertising, labeling and standards. See: www.healthyarkansas.com/rules_regs/food_drug_and_cosmetic.pdf

CALIFORNIA

California Department of Health Services

Food and Drug Branch

1500 Capitol Avenue MS 7602 (PO Box 997735)

Sacramento, CA 95899

Tel: (916) 650-6500

www.dhs.ca.gov/fdb/

The California Food and Drug branch website offers information, regulations, and contacts for all food, drugs, medical devices, cosmetics and certain other consumer products.

The "Sherman Food, Drug and Cosmetic Act" is relatively new (2006) and is crucial for California cosmetic manufacturers. It can be found in its entirety online through DHS. The 101-page document provides provisions for protecting the public with regards to food, drugs, and cosmetics.

See: www.dhs.ca.gov/ps/fdb/local/PDF/Sherman%202006.PDF

COLORADO

Colorado Office of Economic Development & International Trade

1625 Broadway, Suite 2700, Denver, CO 80202

Tel:(303)892-3840 Fax:(303)892-3848

www.colorado.gov

The following web address links you right to the Office of Economical Development and International Trade "Cosmetics Manufacturing" page. Here you will find state information regarding cosmetics, make-up and soap.
See: www.state.co.us/oed/industry-license/IndDetail.cfm?id=140

There is also the Colorado Measurement Standards Act, which has specific packaging and labeling requirements.
See: www.ag.state.co.us/ics/Measurement/MSRulesPack&Label.pdf

CONNECTICUT

Connecticut Department of Consumer Protection
165 Capitol Avenue, Hartford, Connecticut 06106-1630
Tel: (800) 842-2649   Fax: (713-7239
www.ct.gov

The Department of Consumer Protection's mission statement is to "ensure a fair and equitable marketplace, safe products and services for consumers in the industries that we license, regulate and enforce". Their website has useful information on food and standards, drugs, cosmetics and medical devices. This website also links to related Connecticut business laws. See: www.ct.gov/dcp and www.ct.gov/dcp/cwp/view.sp?a=1620&q=273650

DELAWARE

Delaware Division of Corporations
P.O. Box 898, Dover, Delaware 19903
Tel: (302)739-3073
www.delaware.gov

DISTRICT OF COLUMBIA

Government of the District of Columbia
John A. Wilson Building
1350 Pennsylvania Avenue, NW, Washington, DC 20004
Tel :(202)727-1000
www.dc.gov

Online business resource center: http://brc.dc.gov/index.asp

FLORIDA

Statewide Pharmaceutical Services of Florida
4052 Bald Cypress Way, Bin C04, Tallahassee, FL 32399
Tel: (850)245-4292   Fax: (850)413-6982
www.myflorida.com

In Florida, Pharmaceutical Services are responsible for enforcing Florida's Drug and Cosmetic Act. The following website will link you to most, if not all, related documents you will need.

Also, check out the article, "Florida Drug and Cosmetic Act: How It Affects Your Practice." Note that Florida requires inspection and certification of facilities producing cosmetic.

See: www.doh.state.fl.us/pharmacy/drugs/index.html and
www.doh.state.fl.us/pharmacy/ddc-general.htm

GEORGIA

Georgia Governor's Office of Consumer Affairs
2 Martin Luther King Jr. Dr SE, Suite 356, Atlanta, Georgia 30334
Tel: (800) 869-1123   Fax: (404)651-9018
www.georgia.gov

HAWAII

Hawaii Department of Commerce and Consumer Affairs
Business Registration Division
P.O. Box 40, Honolulu, Hawaii 96810
Tel: (808) 586-2744   Fax: (808)586-2733
www.hawaii.gov

The Hawaii Food, Drug and Cosmetic Act can be accessed online. Click "next" at the bottom right corner of each page to go to the next statute.
See: www.capitol.hawaii.gov/hrscurrent/Vol06_Ch0321-0344/HRS0328/
HRS_0328-0001.HTM

IDAHO

Idaho Commerce & Labor
700 West State Street (P.O. Box 83720), Boise, ID 83720
Tel (800) 842-5858   Fax: (208)334-2631
http://cl.idaho.gov

Access the "Idaho Food, Drug and Cosmetic Act" at:
www3.state.id.us/idstat/TOC/37001KTOC.html

ILLINOIS

Illinois Office of the Governor
207 State House, Springfield, IL 62706
Tel: (217)782-0244
www.illinios.gov

The "Illinois Food, Drug and Cosmetic act" is available for review online. See:
www.ilga.gov/commission/jcar/admincode/077/07700720sections.html

Related forms and information for starting a new business in Illinois at: http://
business.illinois.gov/starting.cfm

INDIANA

Indiana State Department of Health
2 North Meridian St, Indianapolis, IN 46204
Tel: (317)233-1325
http://www.in.gov/isdh/

Indiana's Uniform Food, Drug and Cosmetic Act has general provisions for packaging, labeling, manufacturing, processing and wholesale distribution of cosmetics.
See: www.in.gov/legislative/ic/code/title16/ar42/ch1.html

IOWA

Iowa Department of Economic Development
200 East Grand Avenue, Des Moines, IA 50309
Tel: (515)242-4700   Fax: (515)242-4809
www.iowalifechanging.com

The Iowa Drug, Device and Cosmetic Act contains relevant information for
cosmetic manufacturers. Topics are broad; however special attention is paid to
cosmetic adulteration and misbranding.
See: www.state.ia.us/ibpe/pdf/IC126.pdf

KANSAS

Kansas State Board of Pharmacy
Landon State Office Building
900 S.W. Jackson Street, Room 560, Topeka, KS 66612
Tel: (785)296-4056   Fax: (785)296-8420
www.kansas.gov/pharmacy

Cosmetics and drugs fall under the the Kansas State Board of Pharmacy.

See: www.kansas.gov/pharmacy/leg.html

KENTUCKY

Kentucky Cabinet for Economic Development
Old Capitol Annex
300 West Broadway, Frankfort, Kentucky 40601
Tel: (800) 626-2930   Fax: (502)564-3256
www.kentucky.gov

The "Kentucky Food, Drug and Cosmetic Act" can be found at
www.lrc.ky.gov/krs/217-00/CHAPTER.HTM

LOUISIANA

Louisiana Food and Drug Program
P.O. Box 629, Baton Rouge, LA 70821
Tel: (225)342-9500   Fax: (225)342-5568
www.louisiana.gov

Louisiana's Department of Sanitarian Services is primarily occupied with enforcing laws, rules and regulations for maintaining and promoting community hygiene. The food and drug unit deals in drug and cosmetic manufacturing. Important documents can be found on both agencies' websites. Two particularly helpful documents are as follows:

"Basic Requirements for Prospective Drug or Cosmetic Manufacturers" at http://dhh.louisiana.gov/offices/miscdocs/docs-206/food_drug/cos_man.pdf

Louisiana Public Health Sanitary Code, Part VI, titled, "Manufacturing, Processing, Packing and Holding of Food, Drugs and Cosmetics" contains information relevant to this search. However, don't overlook the wealth of information the rest of the document contains. It's available at: http://doa.louisiana.gov/osr/lac/51v01/51v01.pdf

Also see:
http://dhh.louisiana.gov/offices/page.asp?ID=206&Detail=7338

MAINE

Maine Department of Economic and Community Development
Business Answers Program
State House Station 59, Augusta, ME 04333
Tel: (800) 541-5872   Fax: (207)287-2861
www.maine.gov

See: www.maine.gov/portal/business/starting.html

MARYLAND

Maryland Department of Business and Economic Development
217 East Redwood Street, Baltimore, Maryland 21202
Tel: (410)767-6300
www.maryland.gov

Find Maryland codes at this site:
www.dsd.state.md.us/comar/Annot_Code_Idx/H-GIndex.htm

Upon opening the page, search for the word "cosmetic". This will highlight the Maryland Food, Drug and Cosmetic act definitions and statutes.

Alternatively, use the search tool for Maryland laws and codes. See: www.michie.com/maryland/lpext.dll?f=templates&fn=main-h.htm&2.0

MASSACHUSETTS

Massachusetts Business Resource Team
1 Ashburton Place, Suite 2101, Boston, MA 02108
Tel: (617)788-3610   Fax: (617)788-3605
www.mass.gov

Massachusetts has a Business Resource Team. Their goal is to help businesses identify and access state programs and resources that match their current needs. Their online contact form is fairly detailed, and they promise to respond to queries in a timely manner. See: www.mass.gov/?pageID=eoedhomepage&L=1&L0=Home&sid=Eoed

Also, check the General Laws of Massachusetts, Chapter 94, subtitled, "Inspection and sale of food, drugs and various articles". Keep in mind, Massachusetts cosmetic regulations closely parallel federal regulations. The above document in its entirety can be found at:
www.mass.gov/legis/laws/mgl/gl-94-toc.htm

MICHIGAN

Michigan Department of Agriculture
P.O. Box 30017, Lansing, Michigan 48909
Tel: (800) 292-3939
www.michigan.gov/mda

Michigan cosmetics manufacturers engaged in the manufacturing or processing, packaging, packing, repacking, preserving, fabricating, storing or selling any items, must also be licensed with the Department of Agriculture, Weights and Measures Division. Related documents and information can be found at: www.michigan.gov/statelicensesearch/0,1607,7-180-24786_24809-81021--,00.html

MINNESOTA

Minnesota Business Services
180 State Office Building
100 Rev. Dr. Martin Luther King Jr. Blvd., Saint Paul, MN 55155
Tel: (877) 551-6767
www.sos.state.mn.us

MISSISSIPPI

Mississippi Department of Agriculture and Commerce
121 North Jefferson St, Jackson, MS 39201
Tel: (601)359-1100   Fax: (601)354-6290
www.mississippi.gov

The Weights and Measures Law of 1964 adopts systems of weights and measures
for all commercial purposes in the state of Mississippi. Enforcement activities include the check weighing of packaged commodities and testing the accuracy of small scales used in commerce. See: www.mississippi.gov/frameset.
jsp?URL=http://www.mdac.state.ms.us/index.asp

MISSOURI

Missouri Department of Health & Senior Services
P.O. Box 570, Jefferson City, MO 65102
Tel: (573)751-6400   Fax: (573)751-6041
www.sos.mo.gov

The Missouri Department of Health and Senior Services website has a few publications regarding cosmetics manufacturing. "Division of Environmental Health
and Communicable Disease Prevention", Chapter 2, "Protection of Drugs and
Cosmetics," discusses inspection and manufacturing of cosmetic products, including labeling laws. See:
www.sos.mo.gov/adrules/csr/current/19csr/19c20-2.pdf

MONTANA

Department of Health and Human Services
111 North Sanders, Helena, MT 59620
Tel: (406)444-5622
www.mt.gov

Check the Montana Food, Drug and Cosmetics Act, 2005. Chapter 4 is most applicable for cosmetic manufacturers. See:
http://data.opi.state.mt.us/BILLS/mca_toc/50_31.htm.

The Department of Public Health and Human Services also has administrative rules in "Food and Drug Standards". It's long, so start by checking Subchapter 1 for specific cosmetic regulations. Find it at: www.dphhs.mt.gov/legalresources/administrativerules/title37/chapter110.pdf

NEBRASKA

Nebraska Department of Economic Development
P.O. Box 94666, Lincoln, NE 68509
Tel: (800) 426-6505   Fax: (402)471-3778
www.neded.org

NEVADA

Department of Business & Industry
555 E. Washington Ave, Suite 4900, Las Vegas, NV 89101
Tel: (702)486-2750   Fax: (702)486-2758
www.mv.gov

Access the Nevada Food, Drug and Cosmetic Act at:
www.leg.state.nv.us/NRS/NRS-585.html

NEW HAMPSHIRE

New Hampshire Business Resource Center
P.O. Box 1856, Concord, NH 03302
Tel: (603)271-2591   Fax: (603)271-6784
www.nheconomy.com

NEW JERSEY

New Jersey Department of Health and Senior Services
P. O. Box 360, Trenton, NJ 08625-0360
Tel: (609)292-7837
www.state.nj.us/health

The Wholesale Food and Cosmetic Project is responsible for overseeing inspection of firms that produce, manufacture, prepare, store, transport and handle foods and cosmetics intended for wholesale distribution. This is part of N.J. Public Health and Senior Services.

Find additional information by calling (609)588-3123 or at:
http://www.state.nj.us/health/eoh/foodweb

NEW MEXICO

Regulation & Licensing Department
Toney Anaya Building
2550 Cerrillos Road, Santa Fe, New Mexico 87505
Tel: (505)476-4500   Fax: (505)476-4511
www.rld.state.nm.us

Full text of the New Mexico Drug, Device and Cosmetic Act can be purchased through mail or in person. Call for the most recent pricing and payment information.

NEW YORK

New York State Consumer Protection Board
5 Empire State Plaza, Suite 2101, Albany, New York 12223
Tel: (800) 697-1220   Fax: (518)486-3936
www.consumer.state.ny.us/

New York's Food, Drug and Cosmetic Act mimics the Federal Food, Drug and Cosmetic Act very closely. Exceptions and deviations are specially noted in the following document:
www.nasda-hq.org/nasda/nasda/Foundation/foodsafety/NewYork.pdf

NORTH CAROLINA

North Carolina Food & Drug Protection Division
1070 Mail Service Center, Raleigh, NC 27699
Tel: (919)733-7366   Fax: (919)733-6801
www.ncagr.com/fooddrug/

The Food, Drug, and Cosmetic Act is the law that provides the framework used to uniformly administer programs designed to assure consumers in North Carolina that foods, drugs, devices, and cosmetics are safe, wholesome, unadulterated, properly labeled, registered, manufactured, stored, and distributed in a manner that ensures their safety and efficacy to consumers and the environment. Contact the Drug Administrator (at the above phone number) for more information or for a copy of the North Carolina Food, Drug and Cosmetic Act in its entirety.

NORTH DAKOTA

North Dakota Legislative Council
State Capitol
600 East Boulevard, Bismarck, ND 58505-0360
Tel: (701)328-2916   Fax: (701)328-3615
www.legis.nd.gov/

The North Dakota Food, Drug and Cosmetic Act can be found at: www.legis.nd.gov/cencode/t19c021.pdf

OHIO

Ohio Commerce: Division of Administration
77 South High Street, 23rd Floor, Columbus, OH 43215-6123
Tel: (614) 466-3636
www.ohio.gov

OKLAHOMA

Community Health Department
1000 N.E. Tenth, Room 1214, Oklahoma City, OK 73117
Tel: (405)271-5243   Fax: (405)271-3458
www.ok.gov

Consumer Health Services Program has a drug and cosmetic fraud unit whose mission is to provide safe manufacture, processing and wholesale distribution of drugs and cosmetics. Contact them for more information on new rules/regulations for cosmetics and related products.
See: www.health.state.ok.us/program/cpd/info1.html#drug

OREGON

Oregon Economic & Community Development Department
775 Summer St NE, Suite 200, Salem OR 97301
Tel: (866) 467-3466.
www.oregon.gov

PENNSYLVANIA

Drug & Device Program
132 Kline Plaza, Suite A, Harrisburg, PA 17104
Tel: (717)787-4779   Fax: (717)772-0232
www.dsf.health.state.pa.us

The Pennsylvania Department of Health's Drug, Device and Cosmetic Program
has PDF documents available for viewing, printing and downloading. The "Drug,
Device and Cosmetic Program Act" and Regulations can be easily accessed
through this site.

See: http://app1.health.state.pa.us/ddc/DDCDownload.asp

RHODE ISLAND

Rhode Island Department of Business Regulation
233 Richmond Street , Providence, RI 02903
Tel: (401)222-2246   Fax: (401)222-6098
www.ri.gov

Find full index and text for the Rhode Island Food, Drug and Cosmetics Act at:
http://www.rilin.state.ri.us/Statutes/TITLE21/INDEX.HTM

SOUTH CAROLINA

South Carolina Department of Agriculture
1200 Senate Street (P.O. Box 11280), Columbia, SC 29211
Tel: (803)734-2210
www.scda.state.sc.us/

The Department of Agriculture's "Agricultural Commodities Marketing Act" lays
out regulations for packaging and labeling of food, drugs and cosmetics in South
Carolina. Check Article 6 in particular:
www.scstatehouse.net/coderegs/5.htm

SOUTH DAKOTA
South Dakota Department of Health
600 East Capitol Avenue, Pierre, SD 57501
Tel: (800) 738-2301
www.state.sd.us

TENNESSEE
Tennessee Department of Health
425 Fifth Avenue, North
Cordell Hull Building, 3rd Floor, Nashville, TN 37243
Tel: (615)741-7206 www.tennesee.gov

Information related to the Tennessee Food, Drug and Cosmetic act can be found
at: http://tennessee.gov/sos/acts/104/pub/pc0573.pdf

TEXAS
Texas Office of the Governor
PO Box 12428, Austin, TX 78711
Tel: (512)463-2000   Fax: (512)463-1849
www.state.tx.us

UTAH
Utah Business Development
324 South State Street, Suite 500, Salt Lake City, Utah 84111
Tel: (877) 488-3233   Fax: (801)538-8888
http://health.utah.gov/

VERMONT
Corporations Department
81 River Street, Montpelier, VT 05609-1104
Tel: (802)828-2386   Fax: (802)828-2853
www.vermont.gov

VIRGINIA
Department of Business Assistance
PO Box 446, Richmond, VA 23218
Tel: (804)371-8200
www.dba.virginia.gov

WASHINGTON

Department of Community Trade & Economic Development
128-10th Avenue SW (PO Box 42525), Olympia, WA 98504
Tel: (360)725-4000
www.cted.wa.gov

The most useful Washington informational publication is titled Intrastate Commerce in Food, Drugs, and Cosmetics. Find this at: http://apps.leg.wa.gov/RCW/default.aspx?cite=69.04

WEST VIRGINIA

Department of Commerce
State Capitol Complex
Bldg. 6, Room 525
Charleston, WV 25305
Tel: (304)558-2234

www.wv.gov

WISCONSON

Department of Commerce
201 West Washington Avenue
Madison, Wisconsin 53703
Tel: (608)266-1018

www.commerce.wi.gov

WYOMING

Wyoming Department of Agriculture
Consumer Health Services
2219 Carey Avenue
Cheyenne, Wyoming 82002
Tel: (307)777-7321
Fax: (307)777.6593

www.wyoming.gov

The "Wyoming Food, Drug and Cosmetic Safety Act" law clearly defines roles of each agency and facilitates state and local agency partnering. Check the Department of Health Services, a division of the Wyoming Department of Agriculture, for more information regarding cosmetics and cosmetic law.

See: http://wyagric.state.wy.us/ and http://wyagric.state.wy.us/chs/foodsafetylaw.pdf

Glossary

adulterated A cosmetic that a) contains a substance which may make the product harmful to consumers under customary conditions of use; b) contains a filthy, putrid, or decomposed substance; c) is manufactured or held under insanitary conditions whereby it may have become contaminated with filth, or may have become harmful to consumers; or d) is not a hair dye and it contains a non-permitted color additive.

avoirdupois weight A system of weights and measures based on a pound containing 16 ounces or 7,000 grains and equal to 453.592 grams. Informal: Weight or heaviness. (i.e. avoirdupois ounce)

biodegradable The materials making up the item will break down and return to nature within a reasonably short time after customary disposal.

branded shade line A series of products of similar composition, intended for the same use and sharing a common label with the same brand name and the color being only difference between the individual products.

bubble bath Any product intended to be added to a bath for the purpose of producing foam that contains a surface-active agent serving as a detergent or foaming ingredient.

compostable A product or package that will break down and become part of usable compost in home compost piles in a safe and timely manner .

consumer commodity Any article, product, or commodity of any kind or class which is customarily produced or distributed for sale through retail sales of various kinds for consumption or use by individuals for the purpose of personal care or in the performance of services ordinarily rendered within the household, and which is typically consumed or expended in the course of such use.

cosmetic A product, except soap, intended to be applied to the human body for cleansing, beautifying, promoting attractiveness or altering the appearance (FDA)

cosmetic raw ingredient Any ingredient, including an ingredient that is a mixture, which is used in the manufacture of a cosmetic product for commercial distribution and is supplied to a cosmetic product manufacturer, packer, or distributor by a cosmetic raw material manufacturer or supplier.

Cosmetic, Toiletry and Fragrance Association see Personal Care Council

CTFA Cosmetic, Toiletry and Fragrance Association

detergent A cleansing substance that acts similarly to soap but is made from chemical compounds rather than fats and lye.

direct mail cosmetics Cosmetics distributed to consumers by direct mail without involvement of an intermediary sales agent.

drug A product that is intended for use in the cure, mitigation, treatment, or prevention of disease and articles intended to affect the structure or any function of the body. (FDA)

Fair Packaging and Labeling Act An Act by the US Congress to implement standardized weighing, measuring and labeling of consumer products in order to facilitiate fair trade.

FDA Food and Drug Administration

FD&C Food, Drug and Cosmetic Act

Federal Trade Commission First created in 1914, its purpose was to prevent unfair methods of competition in commerce as part of the battle to "bust the trusts." Over the years, Congress passed additional laws giving the agency greater authority to police anticompetitive practices. In 1938, Congress passed a broad prohibition against "unfair and deceptive acts or practices." Since then, the Commission also has been directed to administer a wide variety of other consumer protection laws, including the Telemarketing Sales Rule, the Pay-Per-Call Rule and the Equal Credit Opportunity Act. In 1975, Congress gave the FTC the authority to adopt industry-wide trade regulation rules, including the Fair Packaging and Labeling Act. www.ftc.gov

feminine deodorant spray Any spray deodorant product whose labeling represents or suggests that the product is for use in the female genital area or for use all over the body.

flavor (FDA) Any natural or synthetic substance or substances used solely to impart a taste to a cosmetic product.

fluid measure Stated in Inch/Pound measure as fluid ounce (fl oz), pint (pt), quart (qt) and gallon (gal). Stated in SI units as milliliter (mL) or Liter (L)

foaming detergent bath product Any product intended to be added to a bath for the purpose of producing foam that contains a surface-active agent serving as a detergent or foaming ingredient.

Food and Drug Administration Federal agency. According to their webiste: The FDA is responsible for protecting the public health by assuring the safety, efficacy, and security of human and veterinary drugs, biological products, medical devices, our nation's food supply, cosmetics, and products that emit radiation. The FDA is also responsible for advancing the public health by helping to speed innovations that make medicines and foods more effective, safer, and more affordable; and helping the public get the accurate, science-based information they need to use medicines and foods to improve their health. www.fda.gov

Food Chemical Codex The FCC is a compendium of standards that promote quality and safety of food additives such as preservatives, flavoring, coloring and nutrients. Developed following passage of the 1958 Food Additives amendment to the federal Food, Drug, and Cosmetic Act, to date, five editions have been published (1966, 1972, 1981, 1996, and 2003). As of August 23, 2006 future editions of the FCC will be developed and published by the United States Pharmacopeia.

Food Drug & Cosmetic Act Passed in 1938 (and since updated) with the purpose to protect consumers from unsafe or deceptively labeled or packaged products by prohibiting the movement in interstate commerce of adulterated or misbranded food, drug, devices and cosmetics.

FPLA Fair Packaging and Labeling Act

fragrance (FDA) Any natural or synthetic substance or substances used solely to impart an odor to a cosmetic product.

FTC Federal Trade Commission

inch/pound measurement The measurement system using inch, foot, yard, ounce, pound, etc which most Americans are familiar with.

incidental ingredient (FDA) a) Any processing aid added and then removed or converted to a declared ingredient; or b) Any ingredient of another ingredient or processing aid present at an insignificant level and having no technical or functional effect.

informational panels All surface areas of a package or container that are NOT part of the Principal Display Panel; usually the back and sides and sometimes the bottom and/or top.

ingredient (FDA) Any single chemical entity or mixture used as a component in the manufacture of a cosmetic product.

inner or immediate container The container that actually contains the product. Called the "inner container" when it is held in an outer package; called "immediate container" when not otherwise packaged.

introductory offer Any printed matter consisting of the words "introductory offer" or words of similar import, placed upon a package containing any new commodity or upon any label affixed or adjacent to such new commodity, stating or representing by implication that such new commodity is offered for retail sale at a price lower than the anticipated ordinary and customary retail sale price.

label 1) (FD&C) A display of written, printed or graphic matter upon the immediate container 2) (FPLA) Written, printed or graphic matter affixed to any consumer commodity or affixed to or appearing upon a package containing any consumer commodity 3) (UPLR) Any written, printed, or graphic matter affixed to, applied to, attached to, blown into, formed, molded into, embossed on, or appearing upon or adjacent to a consumer commodity or a package containing any consumer commodity, for purposes of branding, identifying, or giving any information with respect to the commodity or to the contents of the package, except that an inspector's tag or other nonpromotional matter affixed to or appearing upon a consumer commodity shall not be considered a label requiring the repetition of label information required by this regulation.

labeling All labels and other written, printed or graphic material <u>on or accompanying</u> a product in interstate commerce or held for sale.

metric The metric measuring system of the International System of Units (SI) as established in 1960 which uses measurements based on the decimal system (10's, 100's, 1000's), i.e. grams, liters, kilos, meters, centimeters, etc.

misbranded A cosmetic that a) has false or misleading labeling; b) does not bear the required labeling information; or c) has a container that is made or filled in a deceptive manner. If a material fact is not revealed on the label the cosmetic may also be misbranded.

multi-unit package A package which contains an assortment of similar or dissimilar products.

multi-component package A package which contains the integral components making up a complete kit, and which is designed to deliver the components in the manner of an application.

National Conference of Weights and Measures The National Conference of Weights and Measures creates the standards and processes to fairly meet the needs of consumers, businesses, regulators and manufacturers. www.ncwm.net

National Food Formulary see National Formulary

National Formulary Full name: United States Pharmacopeia and National Formulary (USP-NF). An official publication, issued first by the American Pharmaceutical Association and now yearly by the United States Pharmacopeial Convention, that gives the composition, description, method of preparation, and dosage for drugs. The book contains two separate official compendia -- the USP and the NF.

The United States Pharmacopeia (USP), established in 1820, contains legally recognized standards of identity, strength, quality, purity, packaging, and labeling for drug substances, dosage forms, and other therapeutic products, including nutritionals and dietary supplements.

The National Formulary (NF), established in 1888 by the American Pharmaceutical Association, includes standards for excipients, botanicals, and other similar products. USP purchased the NF in 1975, combining the two publications under one cover, creating the USP-NF.

USP-NF monographs contain specifications (tests, procedures, and acceptance criteria) that help ensure the strength, quality, and purity of named items. The USP-NF also contains monographs and general approaches to ensure the quality of compounded preparations. USP-NF monographs, which are recognized worldwide, may be enforceable by the US Food and Drug Administration (FDA) and also by state agencies in the US.

National Organic Program Congress passed the Organic Foods Production Act (OFPA) of 1990. The OFPA required the U.S. Department of Agriculture (USDA) to develop national standards for organically produced agricultural products to assure consumers that agricultural products marketed as organic meet consistent, uniform standards. That National Organic Program and its regulations are the details of how the Organic Foods Production Act was implemented. http://www.ams.usda.gov/NOP

NCWM National Conference of Weights and Measures

net contents The amount of a product left after deducting the weight of the container and/or packaging. The amount of the actual product being sold in a package.

non-toxic A product that does not pose a significant risk to humans or the environment. (FTC)

package 1) A container or wrapping, other than a shipping container or wrapping, in which a consumer commodity is delivered or displayed to retail purchasers. 2) Any commodity that is enclosed in a container or wrapped in any manner in advance of wholesale or retail sale; 3) Any commodity whose weight or measure has been determined in advance of wholesale or retail sale. Note: A package can also include the case packaging of a number of individually packaged items.

PDP Principal Display Panel

Personal Care Council The Personal Care Council is a membership organization that represents the industry's interests at the local, state, national, and international levels, promoting voluntary industry self-regulation and reasonable governmental requirements that support the health and safety of consumers. Renamed from the Cosmetic, Toiletry and Fragrance Association in early 2008.

principal display panel The part of a label that the consumer sees or examines when displayed for retail sale. The size of the principal display panel is determined by the overal

SI Units The metric units of the International System of Units (SI) as established in 1960. They are also referred to as just SI, as in "the SI declaration". i.e. litres, meters, grams, kilos, etc.

soap A product in which the non-volatile portion consists principally of an alkali salt of fatty acids.

synthetic detergent see Detergent

trade secret Any formula, pattern, device or compilation of information which is used in one's business and which gives him an opportunity to obtain an advantage over competitors who do not know or use it.

Uniform Laws and Regulations (Weights & Measures) The purpose of the Uniform Laws and Regulations is to achieve, to the maximum extent possible, standardization in weights and measures laws and regulations among the various States and local jurisdictions in order to facilitate trade between the States, permit fair competition among businesses, and provide uniform and sufficient protection to all consumers

United States Pharmacopeia The United States Pharmacopeia (USP) is the official public standards-setting authority for all prescription and over-the-counter medicines, dietary supplements, and other healthcare products manufactured and sold in the United States. see also: National Formulary

UPLR Uniform Packaging and Labeling Regulation

weight measure Stated in Inch/Pound measure as ounce (oz), and pound (lb). Stated in SI units as gram (g), milligram (mg), and kilogram (kg).

Index

A

B

C

O

P

Q

R

V

W

Z

About the Author

Marie Gale is a handcrafted soap maker and owner of Chandler's Soaps (www.chandlerssoaps.com), located in Myrtle Point, Oregon. She is serving as President of the Handcrafted Soap Makers Guild, Inc. (www.soapguild.org) from 2004 to 2009.

Marie lives in Southwestern Oregon with the man of her life. When not making soap, she manages her family's timber ranch; she enjoys living in the deep woods, but is very appreciative of the benefits of her fast internet connection.

To find out what she is currently up to, please visit her blog at www.mariegale.com.